Microsoft Power BI

Bible

Microsoft Power BI

Bible

By

Jason Taylor

TABLE OF CONTENTS

CHAPTER ONE

OVERVIEW OF POWER BI

In today's competitive industry, data is incredibly important for any organization, and it is more necessary than ever to "know your numbers." If data is represented in an effective manner, it will help firms make decisions in a timely manner. With the use of the robust business intelligence (BI) application Power BI, users may examine an organization's most important indicators. To obtain important business insights, companies employ this application, which creates BI visuals from designated datasets.

Many questions concerning the different licensing options and features offered by each edition of Power BI come up when customers first begin using the program. Choosing the proper license is essential to utilizing Power BI successfully. The fundamentals of Power BI and the capabilities offered by the Power BI interface are reviewed in this chapter. This covers the features that Power BI provides, the different Power BI services, the accessible license types, and the environment setup procedure.

The use of business intelligence expands the scope of data collection and analysis. This section will explain what business intelligence (BI) is and show you a real-world example that illustrates its potential in broad strokes. A broad overview of Power BI and the various features it provides users based on their needs will then be given to you.

BUSINESS INTELLIGENCE

With the use of BI technology, we can extract valuable insights from data that can be examined at different organizational levels and apply these insights to achieve the best possible outcomes. Users can learn and apply the theories and practices that make up business intelligence (BI) to make insightful judgments.

Because BI technologies, such as Power BI, make it simple for users to convert unstructured, raw data into more insightful charts and graphs, BI is a widely used tool for business transformation. Take a big company, for instance, where historical data is kept and presented in a way that makes it hard for decision-makers to comprehend. This data may be transformed into a more useful format using BI, which will provide answers to important issues for the entire company.

POWER BI: WHAT IS IT?

Microsoft created Power BI, a BI application for presenting data in more relevant formats such reports, dashboards, graphs, and visualizations. The data is then analyzed using these to have a deeper understanding of the organization's needs.

The following features are included in Power BI:

- The ability to manage information from big databases, including those that can read a million rows per user every hour
- Dashboards, associated visualizations, and reports that provide data in an understandable manner for end-user analysis
- The ability to quickly identify flaws and mistakes in order to give the end user a revised methodology and approach

Numerous real-world examples illustrate how Power BI can be used to support corporate transformation and growth. Specifically, Power BI dashboards and reports offer actionable analysis to enhance decision-making and cut expenses.

WHO MAKES USE OF POWER BI?

Power BI is used differently by different types of users. One user who examines BI reports, for instance, might like a more sophisticated display of the data—for instance, with color contrasts and characteristics that influence how it feels and looks. A data analyst, for instance, who examines analytics more frequently as part of their daily tasks, would prefer things the other way around, paying more attention to the underlying figures than to the way they are shown in dashboards and related reports.

- Technical BI: IT to the Final User
- Analyst to Everyone: Analyst to End User
- BI for End Users: Everybody

DASHBOARDS FOR POWER BI

Power BI dashboards offer robust dataset visualizations in the form of charts and graphs. These are more interactive for consumers and allow them to immediately uncover pertinent information because they can be studied in real-time from a live data source. Power BI dashboards facilitate user navigation by providing links, or tiles, to relevant reports. It is simple to alter these tiles to suit the tastes of the user. Users can alter the layout of these tiles on the dashboard in addition to adding photographs to them.

PROCESSING QUERIES NATURALLY

Users of Power BI can submit an inquiry in plain English using a dedicated Question and Answer box on the dashboard. After that, Power BI will aggregate, filter, and sort the data to provide a set of visualizations that correspond with the query. Assume, for instance, that a user wishes to examine sales data for their company. Power BI can promptly deliver helpful visualizations to address the user's inquiries.

REPORTS WITH DATA VISUALIZATION THAT ARE EASY TO USE

Power BI may be used to create reports that include comprehensive data presented in visually appealing ways and an easily comprehensible analysis of that data. Power BI reports with visualizations make it simpler to understand the analysis and reach a particular conclusion or choice. In order to drill down for more in-depth information, users create these reports by pinning several parameters to a Power BI dashboard and adding various filters to those parameters.

Visuals including geographic charts, relationship-focused bubble charts, comparison charts (using bar, line, waterfall, and other types of charts), and many more could be included in a Power BI report. You might also think about include comparison charts and other graphics, including pie charts and tree maps.

SHARING WITH OTHER PEOPLE

Unless a particular user chooses to share it, all of their data, reports, and visualizations are kept private. Within Power BI, sharing is simple. For instance, just choose the sharing option from the Actions category on the dashboard page to share a Power BI dashboard with other Power BI users. Alternatively, select the Share with Others option to distribute a report. Next, input the intended recipient or recipients' email address(s) and indicate which permissions they should be given.

Reports with highlights and annotated text can be shared by users to assist end users in making decisions. Additionally, any modifications made to a shared report are simultaneously shown on each user's dashboard who has been given access to the information. Although they are unable to change the report or apply different formatting, users with read-only access can apply different filters for certain scenarios.

REPORT SERVER FOR POWER BI

Accurate reporting at all organizational levels is possible with Power BI Report Server, an on-premises enterprise reporting and self-service BI tool. Other members of the organization can read, manage, modify, or update Power BI reports that users have directly published on Report Server.

With the editing tools provided by Power BI Report Server, users may produce reports that have a contemporary appearance and feel. Additionally, SQL Server Reporting

Services (SSRS) compliant cloud-ready solutions are produced by Report Server.

EMBEDDED POWER BI

With the help of Power BI Embedded, you can share Power BI reports with non-Power BI users by embedding them in emails or materials created by third-party apps. Furthermore, regardless of the dataset selected, data in the form of graphs or other visuals can be displayed in any browser. Current analysis of data created and/or stored within the Microsoft Azure architecture is provided to end users. According to Microsoft, Power BI Embedded will soon be the method of choice for consumers with a Premium subscription.

Microsoft claims that Power BI Embedded has the following drawbacks:

- No on-premises data gateway can be utilized with it. For developers working on particular requirements or adaptations, this becomes challenging.
- Power BI Embedded operates on a totally distinct premium capacity basis, so users with access to Power BI cannot work on the same namespace.

SUPPORT FOR MOBILE

You can use a mobile device, such as an iOS or Android device, to access Power BI dashboards and reports thanks to the Power BI mobile app. In certain situations, analysts can handle small modifications using the mobile app, track data in real-time, and alert users to potential solutions.

Be aware that seeing BI reports on smaller displays can occasionally be challenging; however, Power BI enables optimal display at the appropriate resolutions. To view pertinent information feeds inside the charts and graphs, you can also dive down and zoom in and out.

PLATFORMS FOR POWER BI

Depending on their needs, Power BI customers can select from a variety of platforms:

- The Power BI service
- Power BI Desktop
- Power BI Premium

THE POWER BI SERVICE

Microsoft Azure hosts the free cloud-based platform known as Power BI. There are no internal services or private cloud options for this version of Power BI.

The following features and capabilities are included in the Power BI service:

- The capacity to link to hundreds of different data sources

- An internet dashboard that displays analytics data, such as reports and graphs
- Personalized dashboards
- Personalized reports
- The ability to make changes to reports online
- The ease with which reports can be shared
- Controls for navigation that make it simple to retrieve datasets
- Work areas where people may work together to construct apps using dashboards, reports, and datasets
- Buttons for Home, Help, and Feedback
- A launcher for the Office 365 software
- A box with questions and answers that lets users look for information in plain English

The Power BI Desktop

Similar to Power BI services, Power BI Desktop is located on the user's desktop computer rather than on the cloud. This free tool offers a variety of features to help users create eye-catching visualizations and comprehensive reports that can be published straight to other apps, the web, or mobile devices. It also seamlessly integrates with queries, data modeling, and visualizations for accurate and efficient data reporting. However, desktop users are unable to share reports.

Using Power BI Desktop has the following benefits:

- A variety of data sources are supported by Power BI Desktop, which helps it adjust to intricate business needs.
- To assist users in understanding and gaining insights, Power BI Desktop has an auto-detect relationship option for loaded datasets.
- Creating and editing unique visuals is made easier by an intuitive interface.
- Reports can be saved by users for convenient access. The saved reports have a PBIX extension.
- Users only need one Power BI Desktop dashboard to generate and publish reports.

PREMIUM POWER BI

By expanding capacity-based services to end customers, Power BI Premium offers increased capabilities and performance. These provide as specialized resources to operate any organization's Power BI service. Better stability and support are offered by this specialized capacity.

Without requiring extra licenses for users inside the company, Power BI Premium makes it possible for data to be widely distributed throughout the corporation. A premium workspace is one that has been set aside specifically for that purpose within the company. It operates on specialized hardware managed by Microsoft for hourly bulk data interaction. How many users can access and alter data for reports depends on a number of criteria, including workload and user count. Because of this, the capacity-based resources work in collaboration to handle reports, graphs, and visualizations throughout the full enterprise level

Embedded analytics can be accessed from the Azure API, which offers the flexibility to obtain live data. The Power BI Report Server helps in maintaining BI assets on-premises. The Power BI Premium Report Server supports compatibility with SQL Server Reporting Services (SSRS) to provide interactive visualizations and paginated reports that can be analyzed on-premises. Report Server, which is a feature of Power BI Premium, continuously deploys data from the dataset for enhanced graphical analysis of reports, which may subsequently be migrated to the cloud.

POWER BI LICENSING MODELS

Microsoft offers three types of licensing for Power BI:

- Power BI Free
- Power BI Pro
- Power BI Premium

The features of each license vary. The one you choose depends on your business requirements, including how much storage you need and the total number of users. The following sections explore the various Power BI licensing models.

POWER BI FREE

Power BI Free enables users to generate any number dashboards and reports. However, they cannot share these with others.

POWER BI PRO

Features not seen in the free edition of Power BI Pro are accessible in Power BI Pro. The ability to share dashboards, which allows several people to view them simultaneously, is the most notable feature of Power BI Pro. Additionally, users can work together to produce an infinite number of reports and graphs.The following are additional benefits of utilizing Power BI Pro:

- More than 70 data sources are available for users to connect to.

- Users can examine data in an Excel file or on the Power BI dashboard.
- Content can be synchronized between Office 365 teams.
- Views can be altered by users to suit their tastes.

Individual dashboards can be created by users, which they can save and even add to their Power BI home page. If they have the necessary rights, users can collaborate by accessing dashboards shared by other Office 365 community members. Workspaces can be shared by users. To be informed when shared content changes, users can sign up for email alerts.

- Users can insert APIs into Power BI graphics and reports.
- Reports and images can be uploaded by users to an online platform.

A Power BI Pro license is necessary in the following situations, for instance:

- To post information in Power BI Premium
- To send and receive user-generated content
- To work together on a dashboard or report with other users
- To make reports available on Power BI Report Server

PREMIUM POWER BI

Though it may be scaled for larger enterprises to accommodate more users or to give users additional storage or a greater stream rate, Power BI Premium is comparable to Power BI Pro.

The benefits of Power BI Premium include the following:

In order to support large-scale deployments, Power BI Premium unlocks higher capacity offerings and larger data limits. Reports can be embedded into other applications using Power BI Premium. (Note that REST APIs require a service account, which is available in Power BI Premium, in order to function with embedded graphs and reports.) Reports can be published on-premises using the Power BI Premium Report Server. With data refreshed 48 times a day, dedicated servers enable improved performance.

INSTALL POWER BI

You can create dynamic dashboards and reports with Power BI, an efficient reporting and visualization tool. When you sign up for Power BI, you have a lot of options at your disposal. You can either buy a subscription to Power BI Pro or sign up for a free version. (An additional option is to register for a complimentary 60-day Power BI Pro trial.) All of Power BI Pro's features are available with the free subscription, with the exception of sharing and collaboration tools.

CONFIGURE THE POWER BI SERVICE

Use following procedures to set up Power BI service:

- To access Microsoft's Power BI page, type https://powerbi(dot)microsoft(dot)com into the address bar of your web browser.
- In the upper-right corner of the screen, click the Sign Up Free option.
- Under the Power BI title, select the Try Free button.
- Enter your work email address when prompted. That email address will get a verification code from Microsoft.
- A dialog window to create your account appears. Type the verification code that was sent to the email address you gave in step 4, enter your first and last names, then create and confirm a password. Next, press the Start button.

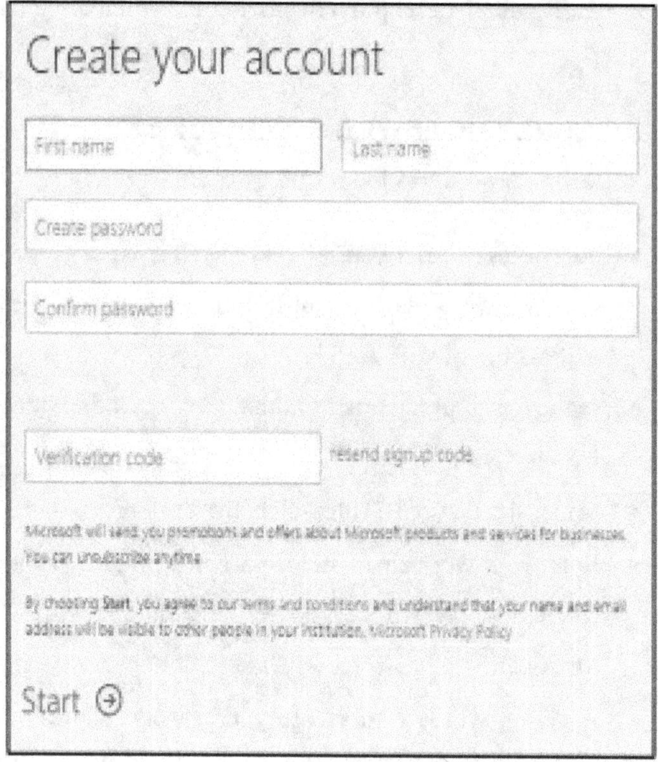

- You get a notice telling you to invite more people in your company to set up Power BI accounts.
- Click Send Invitations after entering the email addresses of anyone you want to invite, if you'd like. Or choose Skip for the time being. A welcome message appears on the dashboard as the Power BI service launches.

INSTALL POWER BI DESKTOP

Your machine needs to meet specific minimum requirements in order to run Power BI Desktop.

**Installation prerequisites for Power BI Desktop **

- Browser Internet Explorer 9 or later
- Operating System Windows 7/Windows Server 2008 R2 or later
- NET Framework.NET 4.5
- RAM 1 GB minimum; 1.5 GB or more is advised. Show1600x900 or at least 1440x900 (16:9) suggested
- CPU: x86- or x64-bit processor; 1 GHz or higher

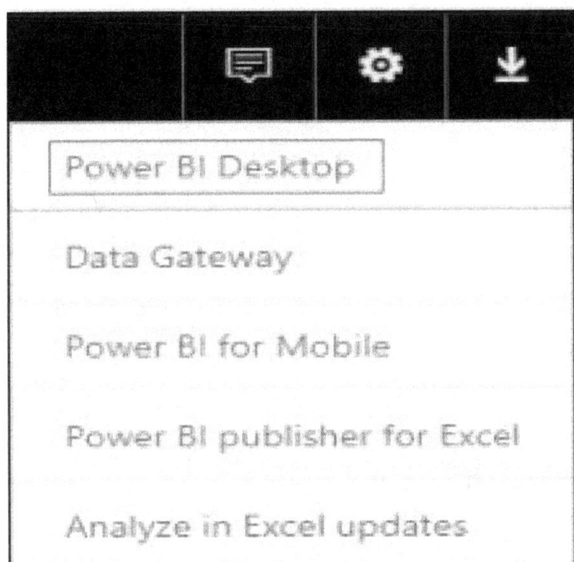

- To start the setup procedure, right-click the installation file after it has finished downloading and select Run as Administrator.
- The wizard for Microsoft Power BI Desktop launches. Press the "Next" button.
- Click Next after checking the Terms and Conditions box.
- Maintain the default file path. Click Next after that.
- Check the box to create a desktop shortcut if you'd like. Click Install after that.
- You can choose to check the item to launch Microsoft Power BI Desktop after the installation is finished. Click Finish after that.
- The Power BI Desktop Sign In page loads.
- To launch Power BI Desktop, click the Sign In button and log in.

INSTALL POWER BI ON YOUR SMARTPHONE

Thanks to the Power BI mobile app, you may utilize Power BI on your phone in addition to a desktop computer. The following mobile platforms support this app:

- iOS (Apple App Store)
- Android (Google Play Store)
- Windows (Windows Store)

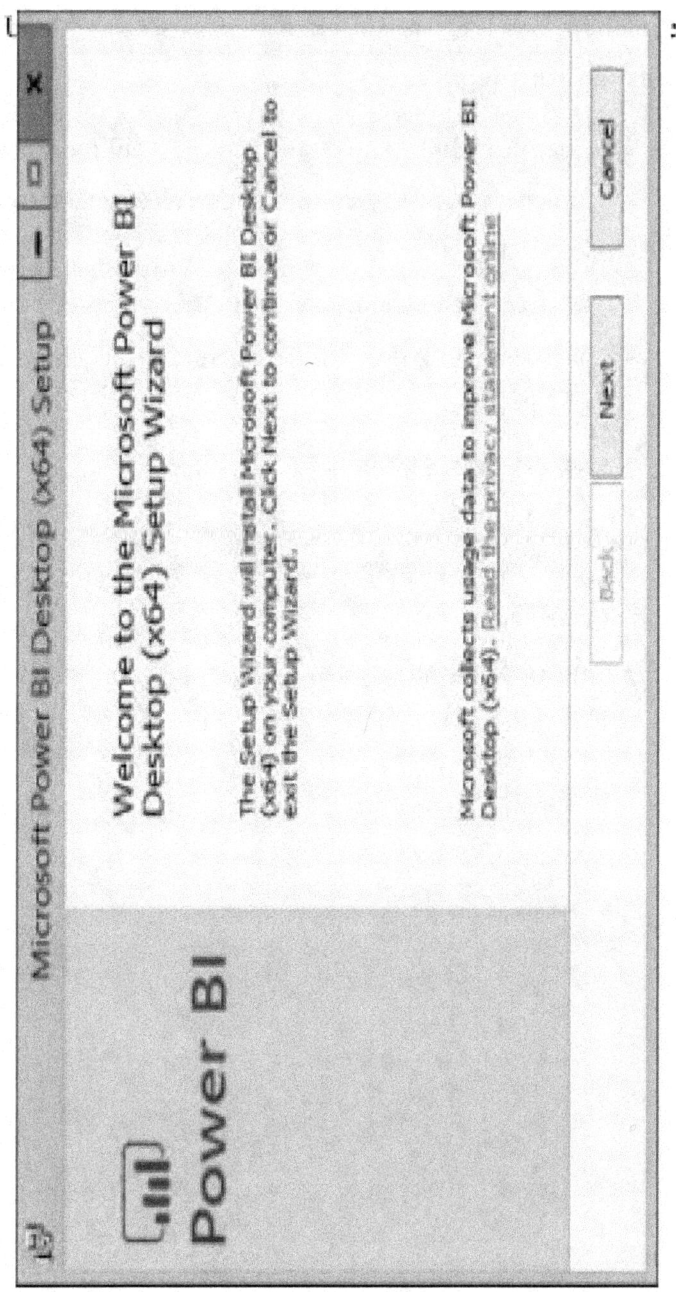
Microsoft Power BI Desktop (x64) Setup
Power BI
Welcome to the Microsoft Power BI Desktop (x64) Setup Wizard
The Setup Wizard will install Microsoft Power BI Desktop (x64) on your computer. Click Next to continue or Cancel to exit the Setup Wizard.
Microsoft collects usage data to improve Microsoft Power BI Desktop (x64). Read the privacy statement online
Back
Next
Cancel

(Installing the program on an iOS or Windows device follows similar procedures.)

- Open the Apple App Store, Google Play Store, or Windows Store on your mobile device, depending on the model.
- Look for the Power BI app from Microsoft.
- To install the Power BI app on your phone, tap the Install button.
- Launch the application.
- Select Power BI.
- Tap Sign In after entering your password and work email address.
- A dashboard will appear.

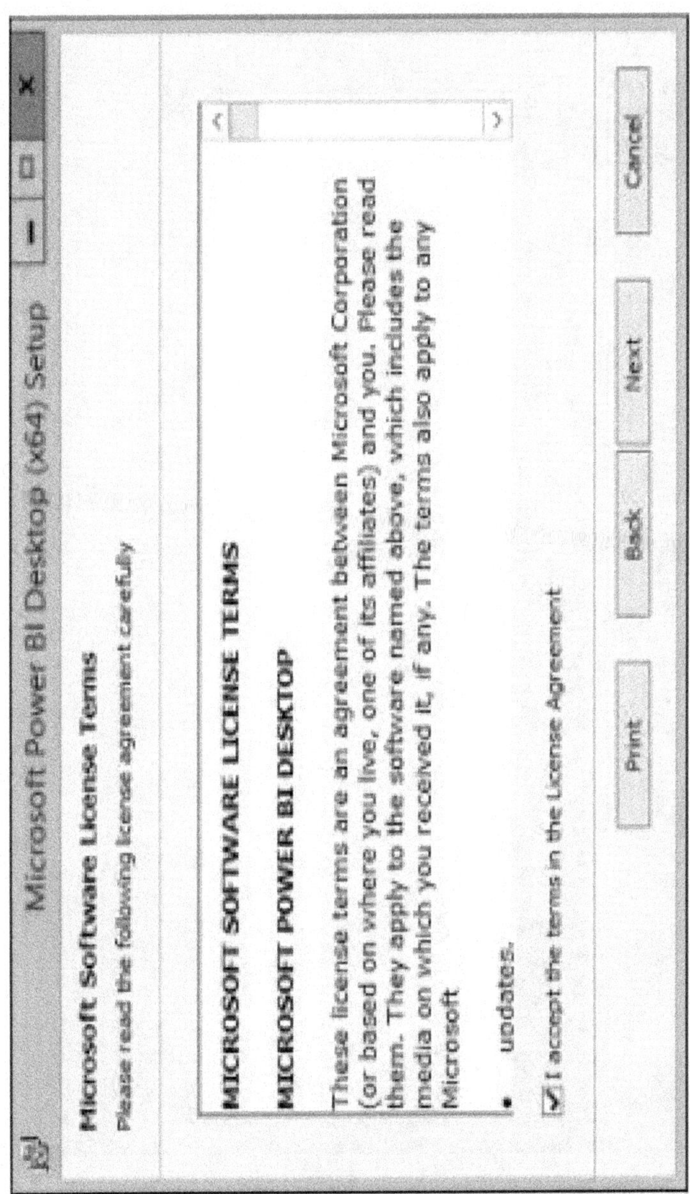
Microsoft Power BI Desktop (x64) Setup
Microsoft Software License Terms
Please read the following license agreement carefully
MICROSOFT SOFTWARE LICENSE TERMS
MICROSOFT POWER BI DESKTOP
These license terms are an agreement between Microsoft Corporation (or based on where you live, one of its affiliates) and you. Please read them. They apply to the software named above, which includes the media on which you received it, if any. The terms also apply to any Microsoft
updates,
I accept the terms in the License Agreement
Print
Back
Next
Cancel

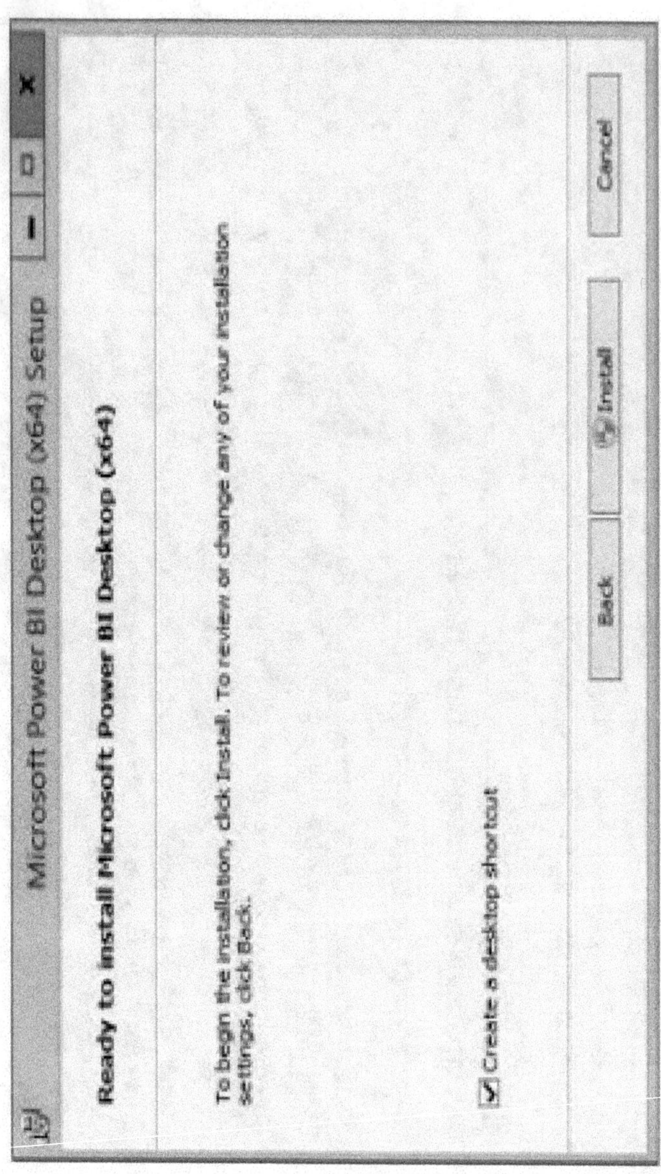
Microsoft Power BI Desktop (x64) Setup
Ready to install Microsoft Power BI Desktop (x64)
To begin the installation, click Install. To review or change any of your installation settings, click Back.
Create a desktop shortcut
Back
Install
Cancel

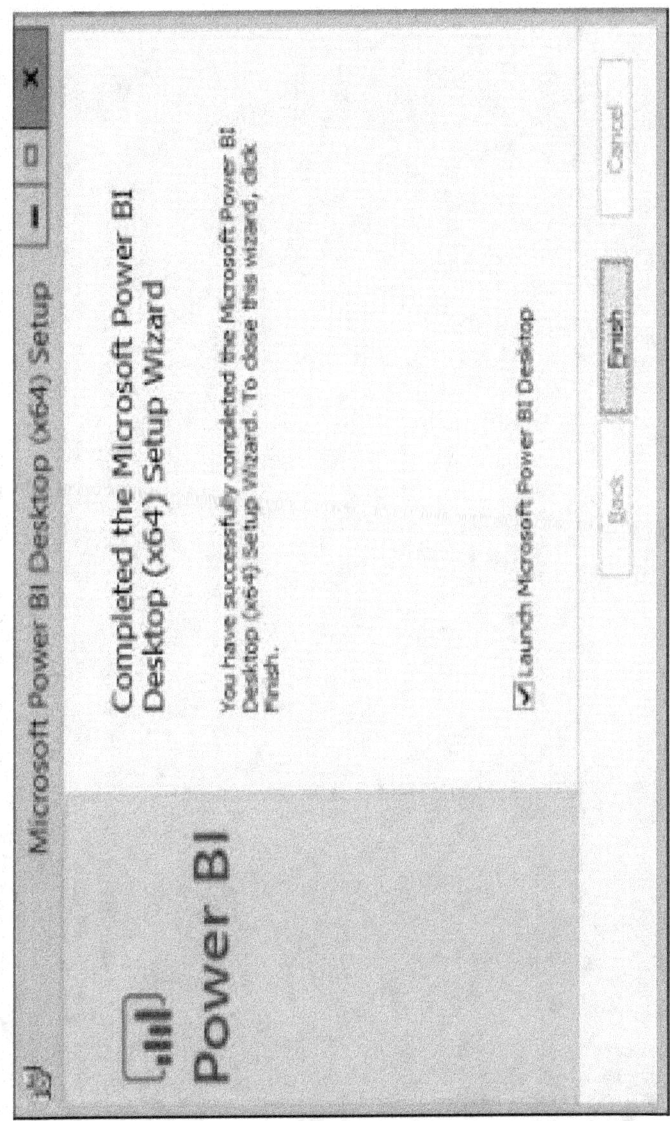
Microsoft Power BI Desktop (x64) Setup
Power BI
Completed the Microsoft Power BI Desktop (x64) Setup Wizard
You have successfully completed the Microsoft Power BI Desktop (x64) Setup Wizard. To close this wizard, click Finish.
Launch Microsoft Power BI Desktop
Back
Finish
Cancel

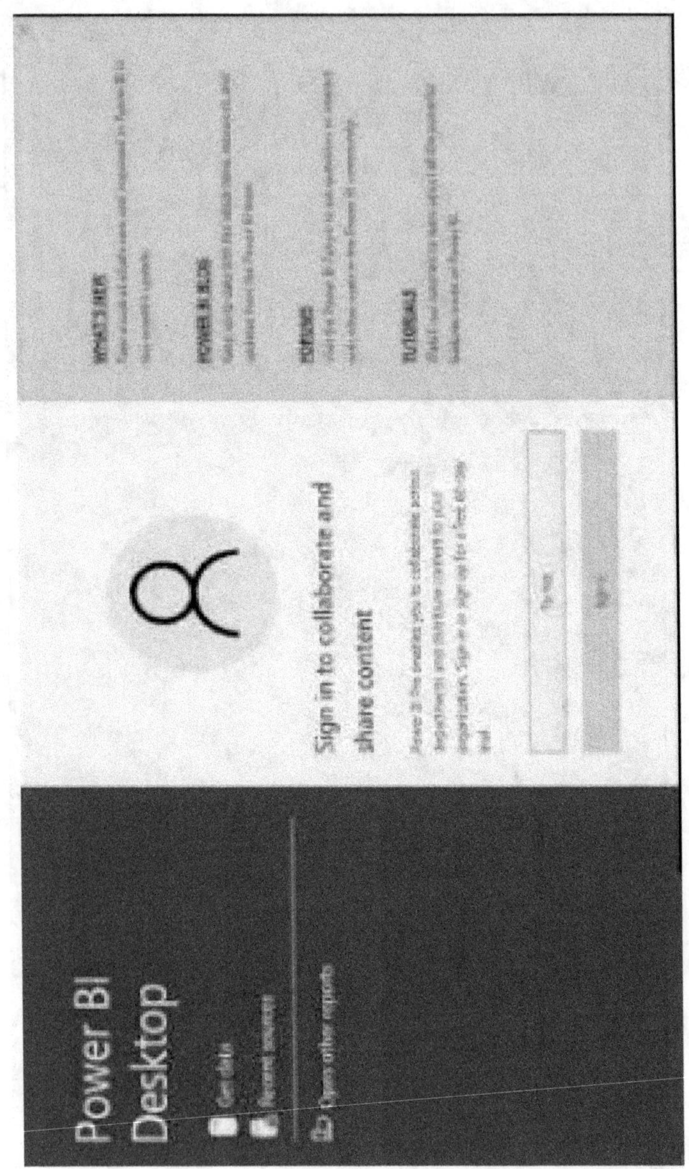
Power BI
Desktop
Get data
Recent sources
Open other reports
Sign in to collaborate and
share content
WHAT'S NEW
POWER BI BLOG
FORUMS
TUTORIALS

CHAPTER TWO

CONFIGURING A MOBILE APPLICATION WITH POWER BI

- Create a Power BI service dashboard.
- Custom dashboards can be created by Power BI users.

This section demonstrates how to pre-pare a basic custom dashboard using a report created and published in Power BI service that makes use of a variety of Power BI service-available out-of-the-box visuals. To create a dashboard in Power BI, take the following actions:

- In the address box of your web browser, type https://app(dot)powerbi(dot)com.
- Enter your work email address and click the Sign In button.
- A blank workspace appears when the Power BI service launches.

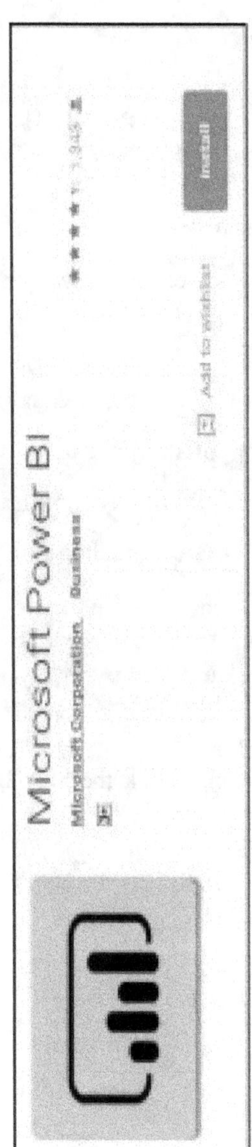
Microsoft Power BI
Microsoft Corporation
Business
Add to wishlist
Install

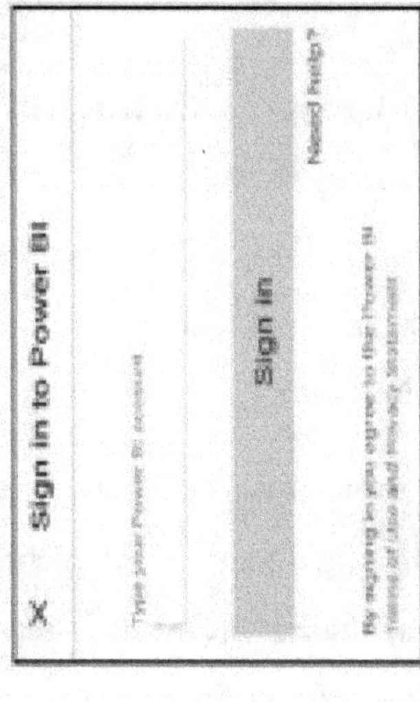
Sign in to Power BI
Sign in
Need help?

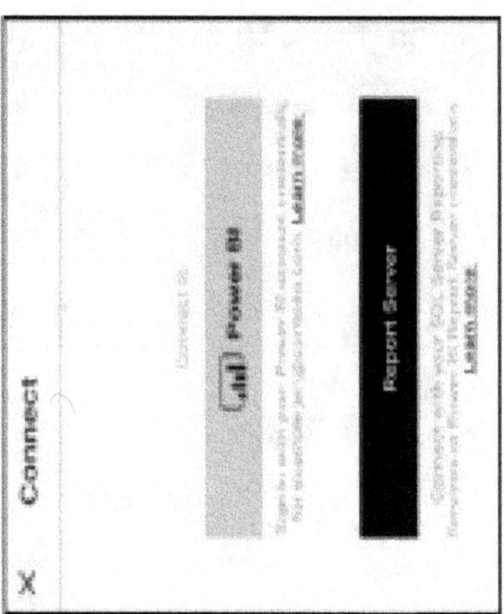
Connect
Power BI
Learn more
Report Server
Learn more

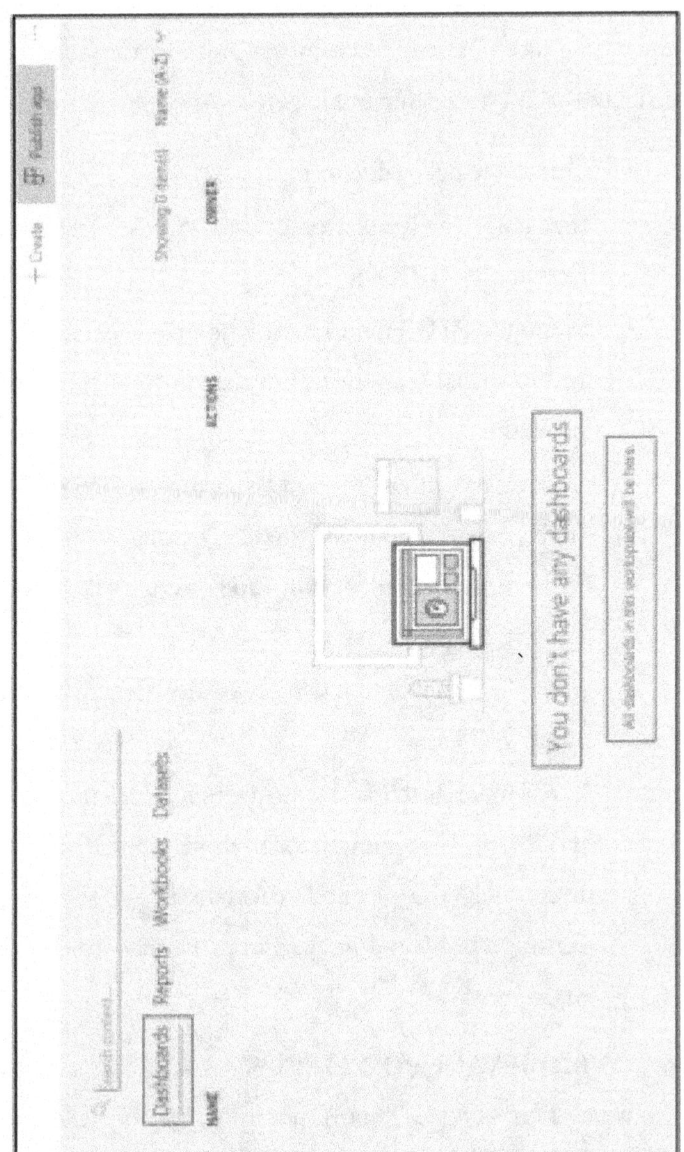
+ Create
Publish app
Dashboards
Reports
Workbooks
Datasets
ACTIONS
OWNER
You don't have any dashboards

Click the Reports option in the workspace and choose the report you like to create a dashboard from to view reports that have been created and published in Power BI service.

- Launch the desired report.
- This report includes two visuals: Sales by Device Type and PTQ Trend.
- To pin the PTQ Trend visual to the dashboard, click the Pin Visual icon located in the top-right corner of the image.
- A dialog box titled "Pin to Dashboard" appears.
- Click the Pin button after choosing the New Dashboard option button and giving the new dashboard a name.
- When the visualization is successfully pinned, Power BI lets you know.
- To add more dashboard visualizations, such the Sales by Device Type view, repeat these steps. But this time, pick the desired dashboard by selecting Existing Dashboard in the Pin to Dashboard dialog box.

AN OVERVIEW OF POWER BI SECURITY

Software as a service (SaaS) platform Microsoft Azure enables customers to create and manage cloud-based integrations online with ease. Since Power BI is based on the Azure platform, protecting it from unauthorized users is not too difficult. The web front end (WFE) and the back-end cluster are the two clusters that Power BI security services often rely on. The user inputs their login credentials through the WFE. After that, Power BI authenticates the user using Azure Active Directory (AAD). The back-end cluster assumes control once the user has been authenticated. Data reporting, dashboard data management, data connection maintenance, and live dataset management are all handled by it. In essence, it manages the entire process from the moment the user submits a request until the Power BI service reacts.

THE ADMINISTRATION AND ARCHITECTURE OF POWER BI

One of the most useful tools for businesses looking to extract important insights from their data is Power BI. Power BI simplifies decision-making overall, increases end user productivity, and boosts data analysis. The architecture and underlying services of Power BI, including the internal and external working structures, are covered in this chapter. It also examines Power BI administration procedures, where a designated user has designated responsibilities to oversee and manage Power BI usage. The report-development process in Power BI Desktop and Power BI service (including workspace capabilities) and data modeling functionality—the process of transforming raw data into a more manageable format that Power BI servers can read.

It's critical to comprehend Power BI's architecture from both a technical and internal perspective in order to comprehend its operations better. This section focuses on it. An outline of the Power BI data-processing model is also given in this section.

TECHNICAL ARCHITECTURE OF POWER BI

We refer to Power BI's technological architecture as the way it takes in, processes, and outputs data for analysis.

The architecture functions as follows:

- Power BI servers gather raw data from a variety of sources, such as Microsoft Cloud sources including Azure data services, Microsoft Dynamics, non-Microsoft SaaS apps, and Excel, Power BI Designer, SQL Server, and other database servers.
- To create a sequential data model, Power BI searches for clear connections between the data entered into the system. (Manual correlations are also possible.)
- The data model is converted into reports and visualizations for end users via Power BI. For other

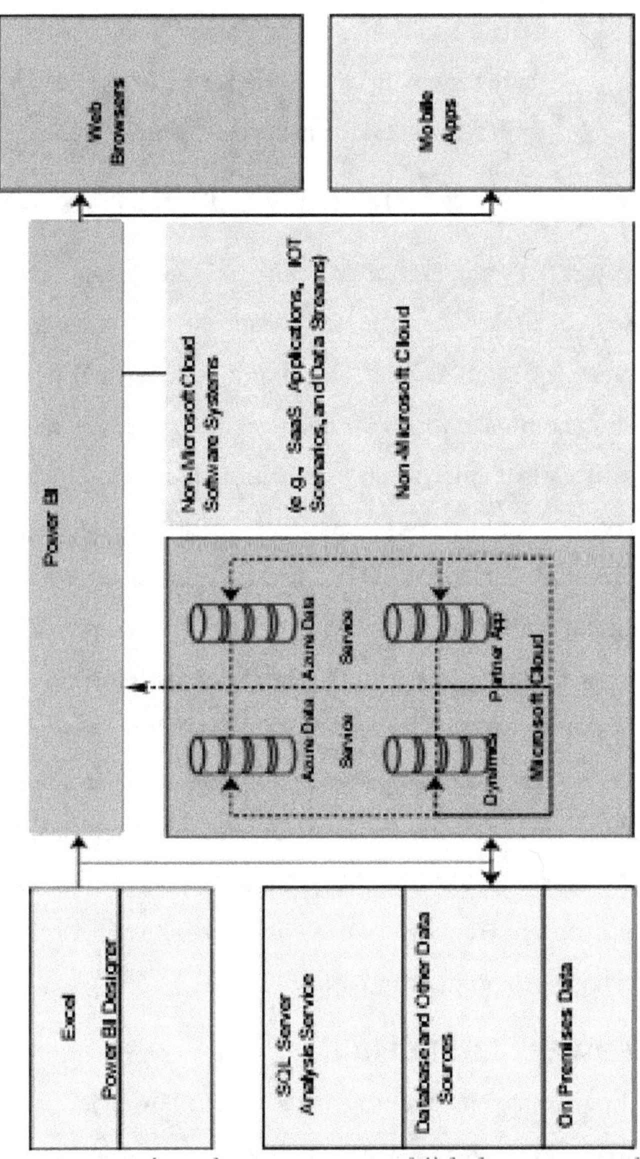

users to view, these users can publish the reports and visualizations online or on a variety of desktop or mobile applications. They might also be allowed to share them with other users for teamwork, depending on the Power BI licensing arrangement being used.

THE INTERNAL ARCHITECTURE OF POWER BI

Power BI's internal architecture is centered on the data sources it uses. Assume, for instance, that you have an on-premises database with SharePoint material that is pushed straight into Power BI Desktop. Additionally, you have data sources that enter your system through a personal gateway, such as on-premises data files, data on OneDrive for Business, data in Excel files, data in Azure, and more. Power BI then filters these data sources for use. Dashboards and reports can be created using the Power BI system using all of the data in the datasets that are available. Depending on the Power BI licensing model they are using, users can share these reports with others and pin them to their dashboard. Additionally, they may access these reports online through the Power BI service or through the Power BI app for iPhone, Android, or Windows Phone.

POWER BI DATA PROCESSING

To guarantee its integrity, the data that Power BI consumes passes through a number of procedures.

This illustrates the following procedures:

- Raw data is read and given a specific data type as it goes through the extract, transform, load (ETL) process.
- The data kinds reorganize themselves to produce a data warehouse or data mart that contains useful information.
- Online analytical processing (OLAP) cubes are produced by the data mart and data warehouse. An array of multidimensional, time-specific data that is processed and stored in order to provide reports and analytical visualizations is called an OLAP cube.
- To create reports, the OLAP cubes' data is input into Power BI and transformed into maps, histograms, graphs, charts, and other graphics.

Three primary stages, or levels, may be distinguished in these procedures and, consequently, in the Power BI architecture.

THE LAYER OF DATA PREPARATION

The system data sources synchronize data in this layer, or phase. Initially, the system-sourced data is available in many file formats. Power BI uses a gateway to process the data from these many sources before integrating it into a dataset. The layer of the data warehouse A data warehouse processes the dataset in this layer by applying filters to it. The data

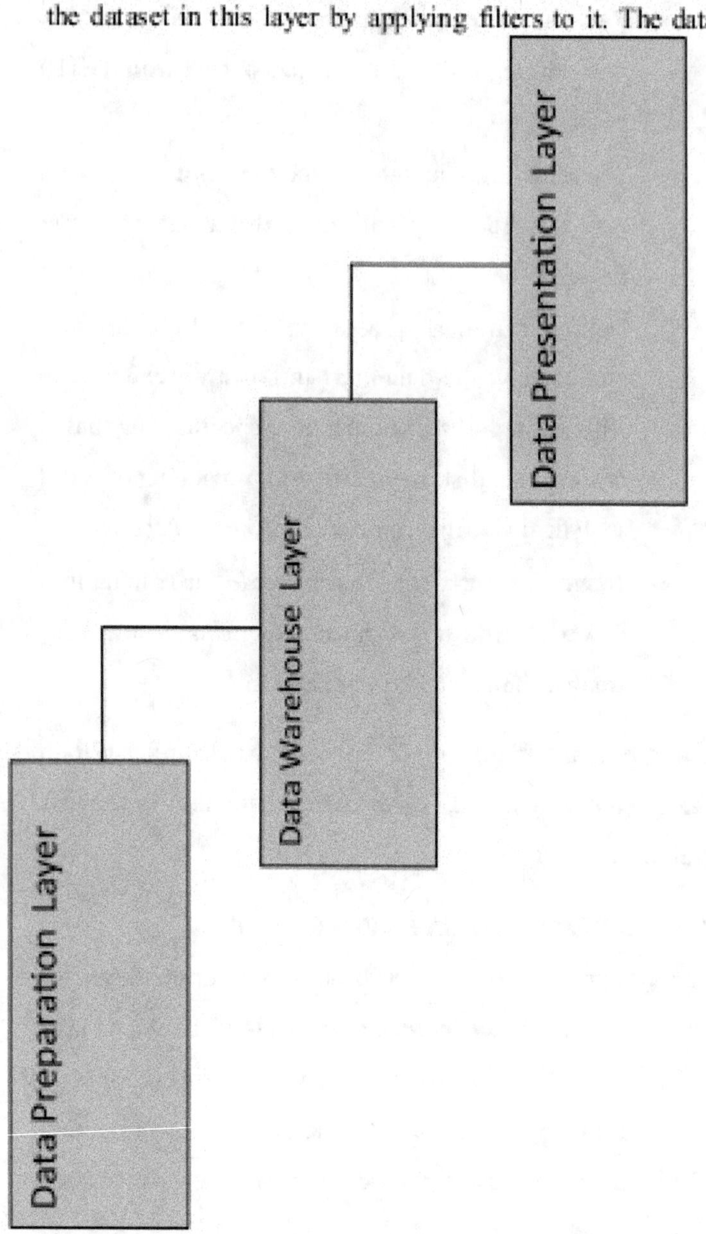

warehouse also use ETL procedures to find errors and fix them as necessary in order to preserve accuracy. After processing, the data is sent to a Power BI OLAP storage unit. The dataset is prepared for Power BI to transform into reports and visualizations once it has been processed by the data warehouse and saved in an OLAP storage unit. These visualizations are available to users on their dashboard.

THE ADMIN PORTAL FOR POWER BI

The Power BI Admin Portal can be used for a number of administrative functions. Take these actions to gain access to the Admin Portal. (Please take note that you must be logged into your Office 365 account in order to complete these instructions.)

- In the address box of your web browser, type https://app(dot)powerbi(dot)com.
- Enter the work email address you registered with and click the Sign In button.
- Select Admin Portal from the menu that appears after clicking the Settings icon (the one with the gear) in the upper-right corner of the Power BI service dashboard. The admin portal becomes accessible.

HOW TO GIVE ANOTHER USER THE ADMIN ROLE

Use these procedures to give various users the Power BI administrative role:

- In the address box of your web browser, type https://portal.office(dot)com/adminportal/home#/homepage.
- The Administrator Portal launches. Click Users and choose Active Users from the pane on the left.
- Decide which user you wish to grant a certain role to.
- Press the Edit icon.
- Click the button for the Customized Administrator option.
- Next, tick the option for Power BI Service Administrator. After that, save your modifications.

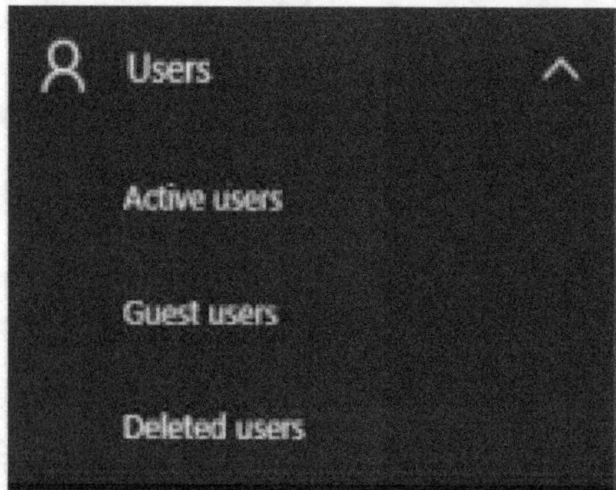

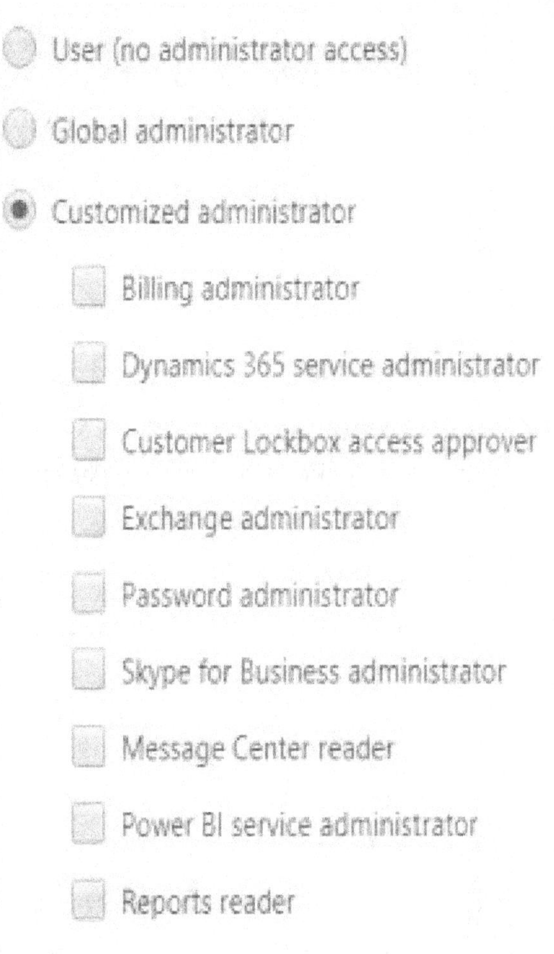

There are various functionalities available in the Power BI Admin Portal. These consist of the following:

- Measures of Usage

- Users
- Audit Logs
- Tenant and Capacity Settings,
- Embedded Codes, and Organizational Visuals

Links in the Admin Portal's navigation pane on the left provide you access to these functions.

MEASURES OF USAGE

The Usage Metrics tab of the Admin Portal displays a comprehensive dashboard made up of various reports from across the company. Providing analysis and insight into a Power BI report is the aim of this website. You may check which individuals and groups are most engaged within the company by visiting the Usage Metrics page. The following usage information is provided for certain users:

- **The quantity of user dashboards:** This displays how many dashboards are present in the user's workspace.
- **The quantity of user reports:** This displays how many reports are in the user's workspace.
- **The quantity of user datasets**: The quantity of datasets in the user's workspace is displayed here.
- **The Dashboards That Users Use the Most:** This displays the dashboards that people have used the

most. For instance, if a dashboard is created, shared by 15 additional individuals inside the company, and its content pack is shared by 10 more, the total number of users who have used the dashboard is 26 (1+15+10).

A group of dashboards, reports, datasets, and workbooks that are compiled within an organization is called a **content pack.**

- **Packages Most Used by Users:** This displays the most well-liked stuff that the user is connected to. These packages could be files, databases, organizational packs, or SaaS content packs.
- **The Most Dashboard Users:** The users who have built the most dashboards (or consumed them through sharing).
- **The Most Reports from Top Users:** This displays the users who have produced the most reports (or consumed them through sharing).
- **The quantity of dashboards for groups**: This displays how many dashboards there are in the group workspace.
- **The quantity of group reports:** This displays how many reports are in the group workspace.

- **The quantity of group datasets:** This displays how many datasets are in the group's workspace.
- **Dashboards Most Used by Groups:** This displays the dashboards that the most groups have used.
- **Packages Most Frequently Used by Groups:** This displays the packages that the most groups have used.
- **Leading Teams with the Most Dashboards**: The groups that have produced (or used via sharing).
- **The Leading Groups with the Most Reports:** The groups that have produced and seen the most reports.

Tools for managing users, administrators, and groups in the Office 365 Admin Center are accessible through the Users tab. Just select the Go to O365 2 Admin Center option on the Users page to get these features. This brings up a page in the Office 365 Admin Center that lists every active user that has the appropriate Power BI administration controls.

ACCESSING USER MANAGEMENT TOOLS

LOGS OF AUDITS

You may access audit logs for a variety of reports using Power BI. Click the Go to O365 Admin Center button on the Audit Logs page to accomplish this. By doing this, you can search for the audit log you wish to view in the Office 365 Security and Compliance Center.

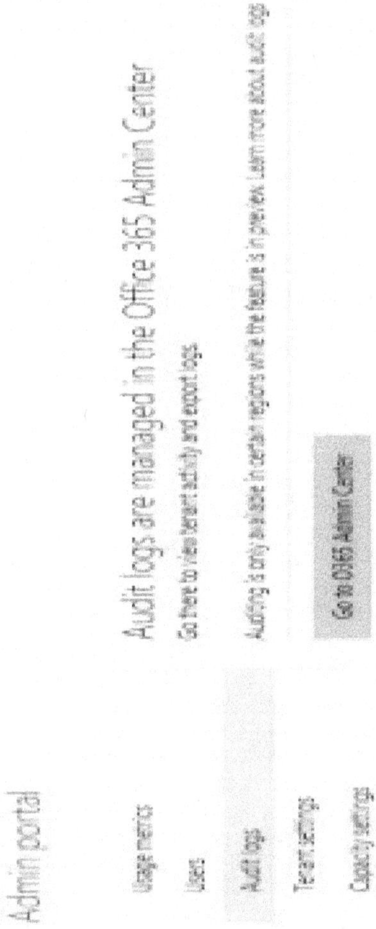

Search

Clear

Activities

Show results for all activities

Start date

2018-07-27 00:00

End date

2018-08-04 00:00

Users

Show results for all users

File, folder, or site

Add all or part of a file name, folder name, or URL.

Search

Results

Date	IP address	User	Activity	Item	Detail

Run a search to view results

Feedback

TENANT CONFIGURATIONS

An organization's users, domains, subscriptions, and other entities are collectively referred to as tenants. By using tenant settings, you can manage who in the company has access to what and make it easier to share sensitive information with particular groups. Additionally, there is a tool that allows users to turn on or off certain tenant-level settings according to their needs.

The following tenant settings are supported by Power BI:

- Export and sharing preferences
- Content pack and application preferences
- Integration preferences
- R visuals preferences
- Dashboard settings, developer settings, audit and usage settings

HOW TO EXPORT AND SHARING CONFIGURATIONS

To control how content is exported and shared, the Export and Sharing controls page has multiple sets of controls. These consist of the following:

Distribute Content to Outside Users: This group's settings govern whether or not employees of your company are able to share content with outside users. Here are your alternatives. Disabled/Activated Toggle this feature on or off by clicking on it.

The following parameters are activated when this feature is enabled:
Enable for the Whole Company: To make the feature available to everyone in an organization, click this option button.
Particular Security Teams: To make the feature available to particular groups inside the company, click this option button.
With the exception of certain security groups: To stop the setting from being applied to a certain group, click this option button.

This group's "Publish to Web" settings control whether or not employees in your company are able to post Power BI dashboards and reports online. The settings in this group are identical to those in the Share Content with External Users group.
Members of your organization can export data from a tile or visualization by adjusting the Export Data Settings in this group. Once more, the parameters in this group are identical to those in the others.

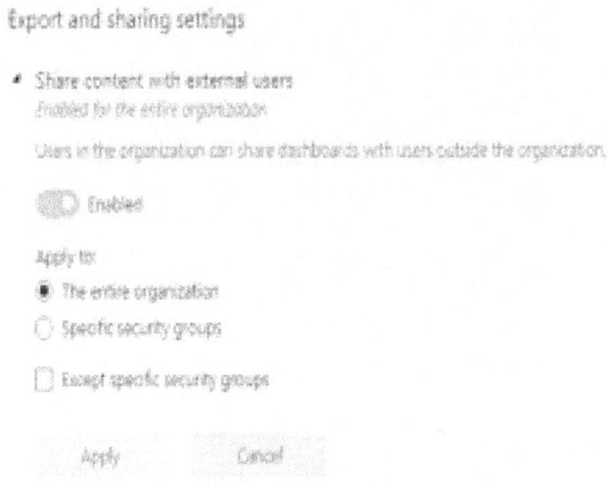

Export and sharing settings

- Share content with external users
  Enabled for the entire organization

  Users in the organization can share dashboards with users outside the organization.

  Enabled

  Apply to:

  The entire organization

  Specific security groups

  Except specific security groups

  Apply Cancel

- Export data
  Enabled for the entire organization

  Users in the organization can export data from a tile or visualization. This also controls the Analyze in Excel and Power BI Service Live Connect features.

  Enabled

  Apply to:

  The entire organization

  Specific security groups

  Except specific security groups

  Apply Cancel

Export reports as presentations in PowerPoint: This group's settings govern whether or not employees in your company are able to export Power BI reports as PowerPoint presentations.

▲ Publish to web

Enabled for the entire organization

Users in your organization can publish reports viewable by anyone on the web. Authentication is not available when viewing reports using Publish to web. Go to Embed Codes to view embed codes created by your organization. For more information, see Publish to web from Power BI.

Enabled

Apply to:

◉ The entire organization

○ Specific security groups

☐ Except specific security groups

Apply Cancel

▲ Export reports as PowerPoint presentations

Enabled for the entire organization

Users in the organization can export Power BI reports as PowerPoint files.

Enabled

Apply to:

◉ The entire organization

○ Specific security groups

☐ Except specific security groups

Apply Cancel

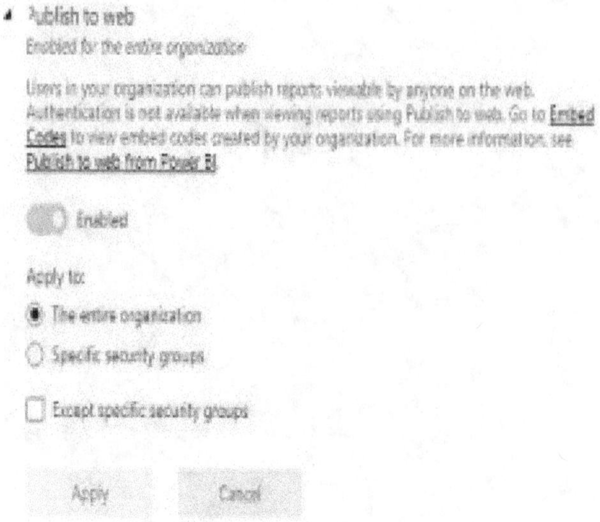

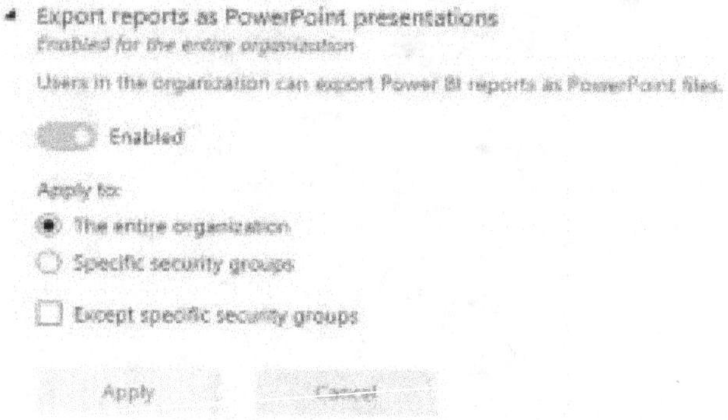

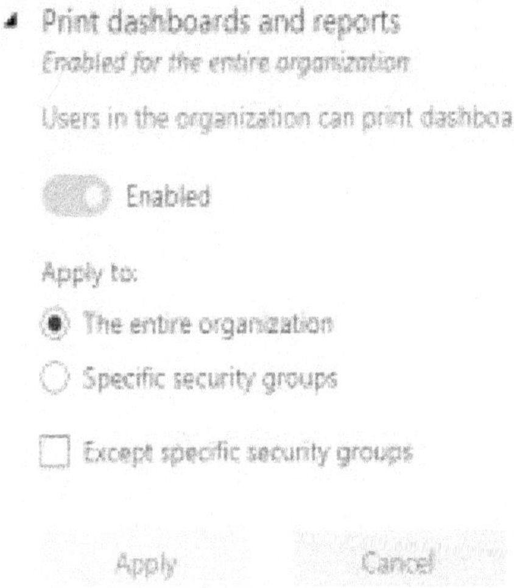

Print dashboards and reports

Enabled for the entire organization

Users in the organization can print dashboards and reports.

Enabled

Apply to:

The entire organization

Specific security groups

Except specific security groups

Apply Cancel

Print reports and dashboards: This group's settings determine whether or not dashboards and reports can be printed by members of your organization.

APP SETTINGS AND THE CONTENT PACK

A content pack comprises all the information that may be updated or distributed across the web or to other applications, such as datasets, dashboards, reports, Excel 2 workbooks, and so on. There are a few ways for handling content packs in Power BI:

- Release Apps and Content Packs to the Whole Company: To enable users to publish content packs to the entire organization, turn on this feature.
- Make Apps and Template Organizational Content Packs In Power BI Desktop, enable this capability to let users construct template content packs using datasets based on a single data source.
- Deliver Apps to Final Users Allow users to share apps directly with others without installing them from AppSource by turning on this functionality.

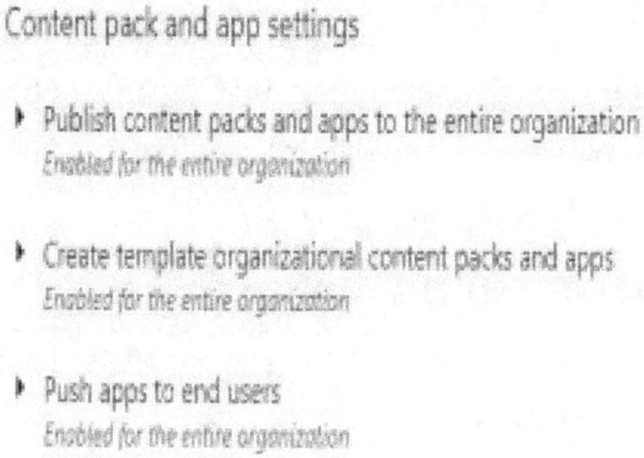

Content pack and app settings

- Publish content packs and apps to the entire organization
  Enabled for the entire organization
- Create template organizational content packs and apps
  Enabled for the entire organization
- Push apps to end users
  Enabled for the entire organization

INTEGRATION SETTINGS

The Power BI Admin Portal integration settings provide users multiple options to incorporate additional tools with Power BI, like as Cortana, Excel, ArcGIS, and Azure to search, ask questions, and analyze data in Power BI reports.

Integration settings

- Ask questions about data using Cortana
  Enabled for the entire organization
- Use Analyze in Excel with on-premises datasets
  Enabled for the entire organization
- Use ArcGIS Maps for Power BI
  Enabled for the entire organization
- Use global search for Power BI (Preview)
  Enabled for the entire organization

CUSTOM VISUALS SETTINGS

This enables you to use bespoke visualizations available for Power BI.

R VISUALS SETTINGS

There is just one setting in this group: Interact with and Share R Visuals. This parameter can be enabled to let users communicate and exchange images made with R scripts. R scripts, often known as R graphics, may display sophisticated data shaping and analytics, including forecasting, using R.

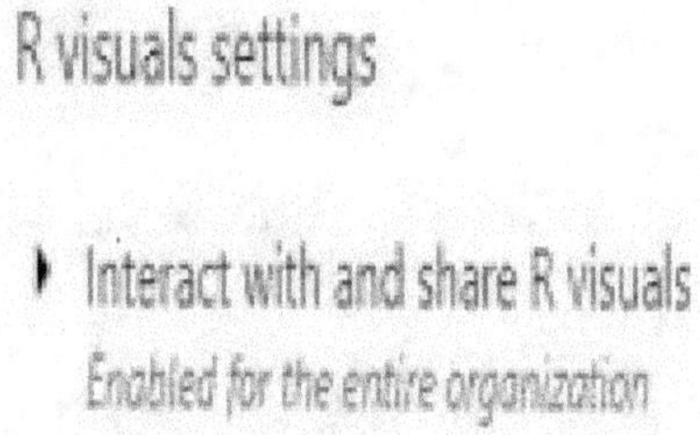

R visuals settings

▸ Interact with and share R visuals

Enabled for the entire organization

SETTINGS FOR AUDIT AND USAGE

Details on utilization metrics for characteristics like compliance, per-user data, report viewing, and internal activity feature are provided by this option.

HOW TO MAKE AUDIT LOGS FOR COMPLIANCE AND INTERNAL ACTIVITY AUDITING

Turn on this option so that users may keep an eye on what other users in Power BI are doing.

Audit and usage settings

- Create audit logs for internal activity auditing and compliance
  Enabled for the entire organization
- Usage metrics for content creators
  Enabled for the entire organization
- Per-user data in usage metrics for content creators
  Enabled for the entire organization

- Content Creators' Use Metrics To enable users to monitor usage metrics for dashboards and reports they have generated, turn on this feature.
- Per-User Information in Content Creator Usage Metrics If you want use stats to reveal the names and email addresses of those who see content created by content providers, turn this option on.

SETTINGS ON THE DASHBOARD

Data Classification for Dashboards is the single setting in this group, as seen on screen 6 in Figure 2-12. This feature can be enabled to let users tag dash boards in order to categorize the data they hold.

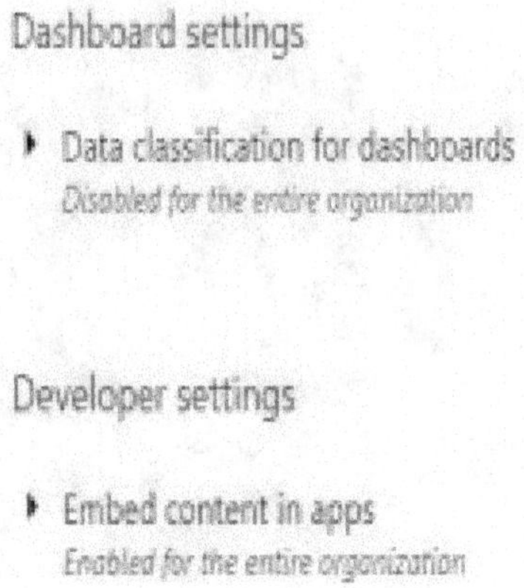

Dashboard settings

- Data classification for dashboards
  Disabled for the entire organization

Developer settings

- Embed content in apps
  Enabled for the entire organization

DEVELOPER PREFERENCES

This category contains only one setting, Embed Content in Apps. Users can embed Power BI dashboards and reports in a variety of SaaS applications by turning on this parameter. This option can be restricted to particular groups or made available to the entire company.

CHAPTER THREE

CONFIGURING CAPACITY

The core of both Power BI Embedded and Power BI Premium is capacity. In Power BI, it refers to the resources set aside for users to carry out tasks like publishing dashboards, reports, and datasets. The Power BI Admin Portal's Capacity Settings page is where you control capacity. You can change the capacity for Power BI Premium and Power BI Embedded. Capacity addition is possible through the Power BI Premium tab. You can access the Azure Portal from the Power BI Embedded tab, where capacity administrators are assigned for Power BI Embedded.

EMBED CODES

The codes created for your Power BI tenant can be viewed, added, or removed by you as an administrator. Power BI report codes that can be shared between applications are called **embedded codes**.

VISUALS OF ORGANIZATION

Users can upload unique visualizations to the Power BI Admin Portal's Organization Visuals page for use by other organization members in their own dashboards and reports.

Additionally, it displays every custom visualization that is currently available for this kind of application.

HOW TO USE THESE PROCEDURES TO ADD A CUSTOM VISUALIZATION TO POWER BI

- Click the Organization Visuals link in the left pane of the Power BI Admin Portal.
- In the Organization Visuals page, click the Add a Custom Visual option.
- The Add Custom Visual dialog box opens.
- Click the Browse button next to the Choose a .pbiviz File box and locate and pick the file containing the visualization you wish to upload.
- Type a descriptive name for the custom visualization in the Name Your Custom Visuals box.
- Click the Upload link in the Icon section to upload the file that contains the icon you wish to use to symbolize your custom visualization in the Power BI Desktop UI.
- Fill in the Description box with a succinct description of the personalized visualization.
- Click Add after that.

- To remove a custom visualization, click the Trash Bin icon after selecting it from the list on the Organizational Visuals page.

POWER BI REPORT CREATION AND DATA MODELS

Preparing the data model for the Power BI service or Desktop platform, running basic operations on the data model, and producing Power BI reports are all necessary steps in publishing accurate and informative Power BI reports.

HOW TO CREATE A DATA MODEL WITH THE POWER BI TOOL

To create more intelligent Power BI reports, data modeling entails condensing content and reshaping data. Thankfully, Power BI simplifies this process. This section demonstrates how to create a data model in Power BI service using the Sales and Marketing Sample Excel file that Microsoft provides.

Use these procedures to create a data model in Power BI service:

- Sign in to the Power BI platform.
- In the Power BI service portal, select the Get Data option.

- Click the Get button under Files in the Import or Connect to Data section.
- Pick the Local File option.
- In the section titled "Import Excel Data into Power BI," click the Import button.
- The import operation's status is displayed in a progress bar. When the procedure is finished, a notification will show up.

HOW TO CREATE A POWER BI DESKTOP DATA MODEL

Use these procedures to get a data model ready in Power BI Desktop:

- Select Import from the File menu, then Excel Workbook Contents.
- To import the Sales and Marketing Excel file into Power BI Desktop, locate it and choose it.
- The dialog box for importing the contents of an Excel workbook opens. Press the "Start" button.
- The import operation's status is displayed in a progress bar.
- A dialog box with the message "Migration Completed" appears when the procedure is finished.

Get Data
1

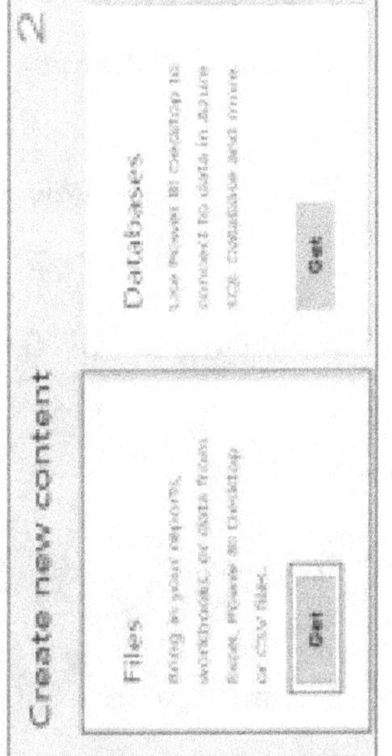
Create new content
Files
Get
Databases
Get
2

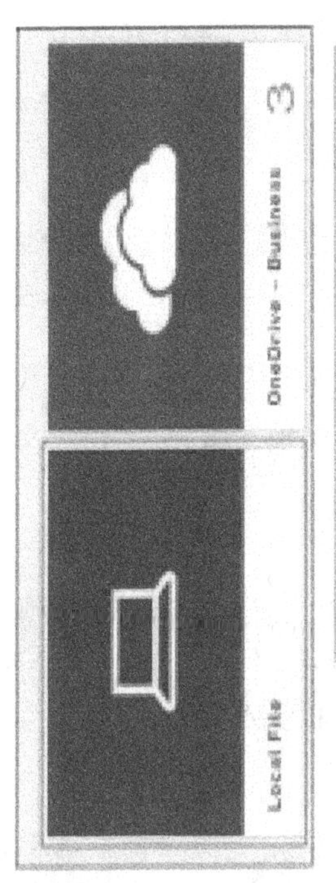
Local File
OneDrive – Business
3

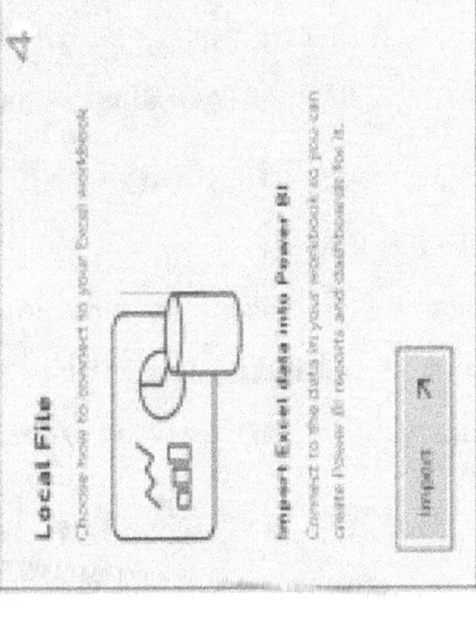
4
Local File
Import Excel data into Power BI
Import

- Press the "Close" button. In a dedicated Data view, Power BI displays the data model, which in this case is the Excel workbook's contents.

EXECUTE FUNDAMENTAL DATA MODELING TASKS

Data-modeling operations come in a wide variety. Renaming columns and altering the data type are two of the most often utilized operations; these are discussed below.

- Change a column's name: There are multiple ways to rename a column in the Power BI Data view. (Once the data has been put into the model, you can see Data View.)
- Double-click the name of the column and enter a new one.
- To change the column name, right-click on it, select Rename, and then type a new name.

HOW TO MODIFY THE DATA TYPE

Both the Data view and the Report view offer a variety of data types:

- Date/Time
- Date
- Decimal number

- Fixed decimal number
- Whole number
- Time, Text, True/False, and Binary

Use these procedures to modify a column's data type:

- Choose the column whose data type you wish to modify in the Power BI Data view; in this example, that would be the ManufacturerID column.
- Select the relevant data type (such as Text) from the menu that displays after clicking the Data Type tab.

POWER BI REPORT DEVELOPMENT

The Power BI version you use determines the report-development process: either Power BI Desktop or Power BI Service.

CREATE REPORTS WITH POWER BI

Understanding how to use Power BI is helpful before you can create a report using the service. The Power BI service panel has two navigation tools, the navigation bar and the navigation pane

Users can access a variety of reports using the options in the navigation pane. These choices include the following:

- **Favorites**: To view reports you have selected as favorites, choose this option. (You'll discover later how to favorite a report.)
- **Recent**: Select this option to view reports in reverse chronological order that you have recently opened.
- **Apps**: To view the complete set of reports and dashboards, select this option.
- **Shared with me**: Click this option to view reports that other people have shared with you.
- **Workplaces**: Click this option to access workspaces that you have access to, like a group workspace or a workspace that you have been shared with by someone else.
- **My Office**: To browse your dashboards and generate and publish your own reports, click this to open your personal Power BI workspace. (Note that this option's exact name varies according on the workspaces you have at your disposal.)

Regarding the navigation bar, the icons in the upper-right corner of the screen are as follows, arranged from left to right:

- **Notification**: To view notifications, such as when one of your two reports is changed or when someone shares a report with you, click this icon. (If you choose the Pro edition, you will also be notified on a regular basis about how many days are left in your subscription.)

- **Settings**: To build and view content packs, manage gateways to connect on-premises reports to Power BI dashboards, and examine data on personal storage usage, click this icon.
- **Download**: To download and save reports from the Power BI platform, click this icon.
- **Help and Support:** To access a help library and user community, among other online help and support resources, click this button. (Note that Power BI developers have their own separate help and support site.)
- **Comments from the Community**: To report problems or offer suggestions for enhancing the Power BI experience overall, click this icon.

The Power BI Desktop: The main interface of Power BI Desktop is more feature-rich than that of the Online edition. The following tabs and functionalities are included on this screen:

- **Pane of Visualizations**: To represent your data in reports, this pane provides quick access to a variety of visuals, such as statistical graphs, pie charts, line charts, bar charts, and more.
- **The formatting pane**: You can use drill-through, report-level, and page-level filters in this pane to apply filters to your data and change the visualization you've chosen. Additionally, this pane provides access to tools for altering the size, color, borders, and other aspects of reports' look.
- **Fields pane**: The active datasets that are available for report generation are included in this pane. Just select the dataset's checkbox in the Fields pane to include it in your report.
- **The report pane:** The user-selected visualizations from a variety of reports are shown in this window.

Several Power BI reports have several pages. Clicking the "+" button at the bottom of the screen adds a new page. These controls can also be used to show a different page. Show tabs You can navigate between these three views on the main Power BI Desktop screen by clicking on the Report, Data, and Relationship tabs.

The menu bar Editing templates, opening new files, adjusting page settings, managing report modeling, getting support, and more are all accessible through the menu bar.

OVERVIEW OF THE POWER BI SERVICE WORKSPACE

The Power BI service workspace has four main screens for data analysis and report creation. Clicking the respective links in the workspace's upper-left corner brings up these displays.

Dashboards Data visualizations, including graphs and charts, are displayed on the dashboard screen. By pinning the visuals they use most frequently, users may personalize the dashboard. Additionally, there are buttons that let the user do various tasks associated with the dashboard they have chosen.

Measures of Usage: In order to measure user engagement, click this button to view usage stats, such as the number of unique users for the days prior and the number of persons who have viewed the dashboard today.

- To share the dashboard with others, click this icon.

See Related Power BI searches the dataset servers for relevant content when you select this button. (Remember that Power BI can also be scheduled to retrieve this data automatically.)

Configuration: To control the dashboard tile flow and Q&A settings, click this. This option also allows you to modify the dashboard's name.

Eliminate: To remove the dashboard permanently, click this button.

Reports: A list of user-generated reports can be seen on the Reports panel. Similar to the Dashboard screen, this screen has buttons that let the user take various actions associated with the report they have chosen.

These consist of the **Delete**, **Settings**, **View Related**, and **Usage Metrics buttons.** The following is also displayed on the Reports screen:

Excel analysis: To download the report to Excel, click this button, which is the second from the left. (Note that Excel libraries must be updated once in order to utilize this feature.)

Fast Insights: To rapidly extract important insights from a report, click this button (third from the left) to see a list of all the visualizations that are accessible. Any important visualizations can then be pinned to the dashboard.

WORKBOOKS

Excel files can be uploaded to Power BI. They show up in the Workbooks screen when you do that. The Workbooks screen has buttons to execute various tasks on the selected workbook, same like the other screens.

- **Refresh**: To update the data in the chosen Excel file, click this button.
- **Substitute**: Click this button to switch out the Excel file that is now chosen.
- **Configuration**: To modify the Excel file's name and view its location on the local server, click this button to enter the settings.
- **Delete**: To remove the Excel file, click this button.

DATASETS

The datasets for every report the user has prepared are listed on this screen. You can do various actions on the chosen dataset by using the buttons on the Datasets screen, just like on the other screens.

Make a report: To generate a new report using the chosen dataset, click this button.

Refresh: In order to refresh the dataset, click this button. **Refresh the Schedule**: To plan a dataset refresh, click this button.

See Related: Related datasets can be found by clicking this button.

HOW TO MODIFY POWER BI SERVICE CHOICES

The Power BI service's menu bar provides buttons and menus with a number of important settings. These consist of the following:

The following commands are included in this menu:

- Download Report
- Save As
- Print
- Publish to Web
- Embedded in SharePoint Online
- Export to PowerPoint

The following Power BI report view options are available through this menu:

- Fit to width
- Fit to page and actual size

Edit the report: To edit your report, go and access the editing tools.

Investigate: Options for exploring through datasets are thus made available.

Refresh: In order to refresh the selected report, click its button.

Pin Live Page: To pin the current page of the chosen report to your dashboard, click this option.

See Related: To see how your Power BI service content—that is, your dashboards, reports, and datasets—are connected, choose this option to open the Related Content window.

Sign up: To get email alerts when the current Power BI report page changes, click this button. (Emails can only be sent once a day, provided the report has been updated.)

Create a QR Code: To generate a report-specific QR code that is accessible from a mobile device, click this button.

View in Excel: To view the report in tabular form in Microsoft Excel, click its button.

File
View
Edit report
Refresh
Pin Live Page
View related
Favorite
Subscribe
Share
Generate QR code
Analyze in Excel

POWER BI VISUAL GRAPHICS

Visuals are a vital feature of Power BI. Understanding them is vital to correctly integrating them in reports. This section discusses the characteristics and benefits of several Power BI graphics.

WHAT ARE VISUALS?

A visual, or visualization, is a graphical depiction of data in the form of a chart, graph, or map, which allows end users to understand information in its simplest form. Visualizations help decision-makers to assess components of the data that are critical for organizational growth. With Power BI, graphically visualizing data is easy and uncomplicated, making it much easier to absorb the available information.

BENEFITS OF UTILIZING POWER BI VISUALIZATIONS

Benefits of utilizing Power BI visualizations include the following:

- Power BI delivers several graphics out of the box, which makes report development very straightforward. You merely need to drag the graphic to the report and add the appropriate fields.
- You may apply filters at the visual level, page level, or report level, to make the report more relevant for

consumers. (For more on filters, see the forthcoming section, "Apply filters in Power BI reports.")

- You can utilize the R-Script Editor in Power BI to generate bespoke visualizations. (Note that to use this function, you must install R on your local system.)
- You may share visuals in reports or on dashboards with colleagues in your business (provided you have a Power BI Pro subscription).

POWER BI VISUALIZATIONS OUT OF THE BOX

Power BI Desktop includes OOTB graphics, with updated and new visuals published by Microsoft on a regular basis. These OOTB graphics include the following:

- Bar charts
- Column charts
- Line charts
- Area charts
- Line and stacked column charts
- Ribbon charts
- Waterfall charts
- Scatter charts
- Donut charts
- Funnel charts

- Gauge charts
- KPI visuals
- Tables
- Matrix visuals
- Bubble charts
- Cards
- Maps
- Pie charts
- Multi-row card
- ArcGIS maps

BAR, COLUMN, AND RIBBON CHARTS

When you have categorical data, then a bar or column chart is an ideal approach to present it. Bar charts represent data horizontally, whereas column charts depict information vertically. Bar and column charts are commonly utilized in companies. Indeed, you'll often find that bar and column charts cover 70% of most simple dashboards.

Suppose you are dealing with a vast database of information from a single hospital. The database contains tons of heterogeneous data containing specifics about the hospital's patients, including their age. If, for example, you wanted to construct a graphic depicting the age split of the hospital's patients, a bar or column chart may be a decent selection.

Power BI supports the following styles of bar and column charts out of the box:

- **Stacked bar charts**: This style of chart is beneficial if you need to know both the values of numerous subcategories of data as well as the overall value.
- **Clustered bar charts:** This sort of chart presents a comparison of all categories and subcategories as a component of a whole.
- **100% stacked bar charts**: Like a typical stacked bar chart, a 100% stacked bar chart combines several subcategories of data into a single bar. However, it is displayed as a percentage.
- **Stacked, clustered, and 100% stacked column charts:** These are much like their bar chart cousins, except turned on their side, so the bars are vertical rather than horizontal.
- **Ribbon charts:** These are similar to stacked column charts but depict each category according to rank or value.

LINE, AREA, AND COMBINATION CHARTS

Line, area, and combination charts are effective for depicting data that varies over time, whereas ribbon charts are merely a variant on column charts.

- **Line charts:** They are important for time-based data—for example, if you need to study sales data for a manufacturing business, including their unit budget, quota, and quantities, over certain time
- **Area charts:** An area chart is a form of line chart. Unlike line charts, however, which merely illustrate continuous development over a period of time, area charts also reflect volume.
- **Stacked area charts**: These are similar to area charts but present the data in a stacked style, enabling you to understand how each category contributes to the overall.
- **Line and stacked column charts**: This style of chart is a mix of a line chart and a stacked column chart. You may use a line and stacked column chart if, for example, you had school data, and you wanted to display how many days children in each grade were present and absent during a given time.
- **Line and clustered column charts:** This style of chart is a mix of a line chart and a clustered column

chart. You may use a line and clustered column chart in the same circumstance as you would a line and stacked column chart.

WATERFALL, TREEMAP, SCATTER, BUBBLE, PIE, DONUT, FUNNEL, AND GAUGE CHARTS

Power BI features numerous additional specialized charts for usage in reports and dashboards:

- **Waterfall charts:** This style of chart illustrates changes in a value over time. It's useful when you need to maintain a running total.
- **Treemaps**: A treemap depicts data as rectangles in hierarchical order. Treemaps often illustrate proportions in various colors and sizes to assist users to more readily interpret enormous amounts of data. This sort of chart is helpful when data comprises several subcategories that are difficult to analyze in bar charts.
- **Scatter charts**: This sort of chart contains a horizontal and a vertical axis to represent numerical values, enabling you to depict at least two sets of numbers as a sequence of XY coordinates. An example of a case in which a scatter chart can be beneficial is if you want to illustrate yearly sales data

by variance of total sales and by sales value per square foot.

- **Bubble charts**: This style of chart presents data in the shape of bubbles, with the size of the bubble indicating the data value. Bubble charts are typically used in the same sorts of circumstances as scatter charts.
- **Pie charts:** A pie chart is a circular statistical depiction of data that is split into slices to indicate proportion or percentage.
- **Donut charts:** These are similar to pie charts, but with circular part taken off in the middle.
- Funnel charts: This sort of chart presents linear data with consecutive linked phases, with each funnel stage representing a proportion of the overall. It is widely used to assess sales-conversion data throughout a business.
- **Gauge charts:** A gauge chart presents data in an arc to demonstrate progress toward a goal. The left side of the arc represents the least value, while the right side shows the greatest value.

CARDS, MULTI-ROW CARDS, AND KPI VISUALIZATIONS

In addition to the charts and graphs already covered, Power BI supports more forms of graphics, including the following:

- **Cards**: These are used to represent a single value of data examined according to specific parameters specified.
- **Multi-row cards**: These exhibit numerous rows of facts in a single card sheet to aid users to arrive at a given conclusion.
- **KPI visuals**: A key performance indicator (KPI) graphic measures the progress of progress toward a specific objective. It tells if you are behind, on track, or ahead of the game.

TABLE AND MATRIX VISUALIZATIONS

Tables and matrixes are further types of graphics in Power BI.

- **Tables**: This style of graphic is best suited for numbers in tabular format rep- resenting specific classes of data gathered together. Tables, which allow for conditional formatting, promote quick and fast group analysis.

- **Matrix:** Matrix graphics provide for tabular representation of data with drill-down features, enabling you to incorporate more rows or columns or a particular portion.

BUBBLE, FILLED, AND ARCGIS MAPS

Power BI enables the usage of the following map visuals:

- **Bubble maps**: This graphic overlays data in the form of a bubble on a geographical map created by Bing using location information you give. The size of the bubble over a certain geographic location indicates the data value
- **Filled maps**: This depicts data inside geographic regions on a map (again, generated by Bing using location information you supply) rather than as an isolated point, with lighter colors indicating lower values and deeper shades suggesting greater values. Filled maps offer an overview of data distribution throughout a location, such as a nation, state, or city, and are an excellent method to highlight linkages among data and to check for spatial patterns.
- **ArcGIS maps**: Although these maps are provided by a third-party provider, ESRI, they are offered in Power BI out of the box. They enable you to

designate precise regions and present viewers with rich graphical material. Users may zoom in, zoom out, and choose one or many destinations. When you add data to the map, it is automatically customized as needed. These maps are incredibly valuable for users that need to see data spatially.

VISUALS FROM THIRD PARTIES IN POWER BI

Power BI has a number of helpful graphics. However, you may download and import a number of third-party visualizations into Power BI if none of these ones satisfy your needs. These images can be obtained in two ways:

- By importing a third-party visual file into Power BI after getting it from the Microsoft AppSource
- By using the Import option in Power BI to directly access the Microsoft AppSource

A third-party graphic file should be downloaded and imported into Power BI.

HOW TO IMPORT A THIRD-PARTY VISUAL

Use these procedures to import a third-party graphic into Power BI after downloading it from the Microsoft AppSource:

- In the URL bar of your web browser, type https://appsource(dot)microsoft(dot)com/en-us/marketplace/apps?page=1&product=power-bi-visuals.
- Microsoft AppSource becomes accessible.
- Click Get It Now next to the third-party image you wish to download.
- When prompted, provide your Power BI password and work email address, then click Keep agreeing to the terms and conditions.
- A PBVIZ file will be downloaded by Power BI Desktop.
- Select Import from File by clicking the ... link in the Visualizations tab of Power BI Desktop.
- A Warning: The dialog box to import custom visuals opens.
- Press the "Import" button.
- Click Import after finding and selecting the recently downloaded file.
- Following the import process, the following notice will appear: This report's graphic was successfully imported. You may then choose the graphic from the Visualizations window.

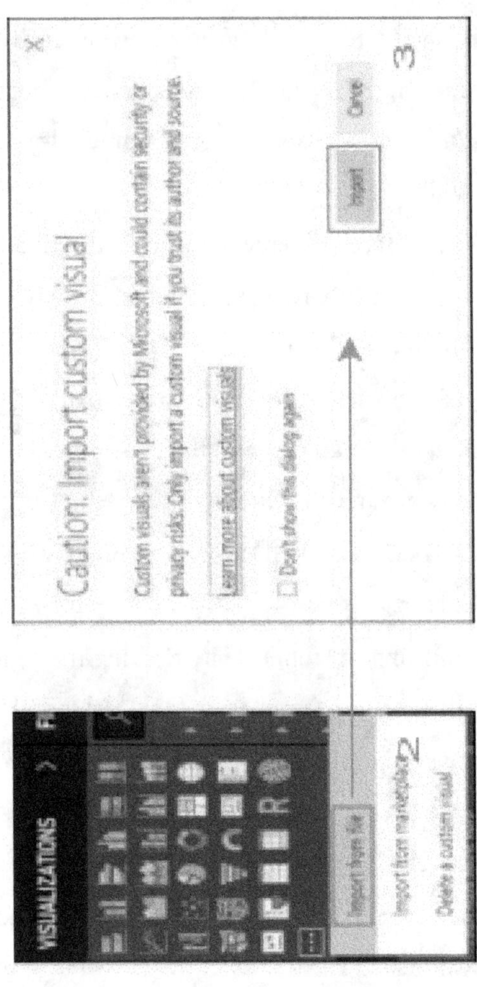
Caution: Import custom visual
Custom visuals aren't provided by Microsoft and could contain security or privacy risks. Only import a custom visual if you trust its author and source.
Learn more about custom visuals
Don't show this dialog again
Import
Cancel
3
VISUALIZATIONS
Import from file
Import from marketplace
2
Delete a custom visual

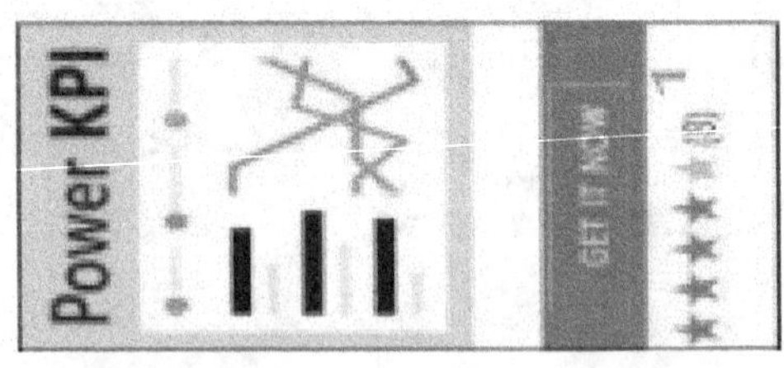
Power KPI
GET IT NOW
(9)
1

HOW TO IMPORT AN IMAGE FROM A THIRD PARTY

To import an image from a third party, go straight to the Microsoft AppSource. To import a third-party graphic straight from Power BI, use the following steps to access the Microsoft AppSource:

- Select Import from Marketplace by clicking the link in the Visualizations tab of Power BI Desktop.
- A collection of third-party images appears when the Microsoft AppSource opens.
- Click the Add button after selecting a picture.
- Following the import process, the following notice will appear: This report's graphic was successfully imported. The graphic may then be chosen from the Visualizations window.

Power BI visualizations make it possible to create visually appealing reports. Users may examine the data much more easily as a result, and potential mistakes are decreased. It is helpful to conceive of data in Power BI graphics as residing in a hierarchy of sorts. In order to obtain more insights while working with Power BI graphics, this section explains the tools you may use to dive into that hierarchy. Drill down Subsets of information may be included in each data point in a visualization, which might offer further understanding. Consider a graphic that displays the number of patients enrolled in different hospital programs, for instance. You may learn more about these patients, including their age, gender, and other details, by selecting the Drill Down option

HOW TO USE FILTERS WHILE CREATING POWER BI REPORTS

Take Things to the Next Level Click the Expand to Next Level button to dig down all fields simultaneously by one level. This displays every field that is available in the following hierarchy. Assume, for instance, that you have a graphic that shows postal code information along with information about the nation, state, and province. Assume further that the graphic includes information on the United States and Canada.

The image will alter to display all three provinces and states in the US and Canada if you select Expand to Next Level. The image will reload with all of the postal codes for every state and province if you click it again. Get Drilling You may go back up one level by clicking Drill after selecting Drill

Down or Expand to Next Level. Expand Down Select this option to extend all levels at once.

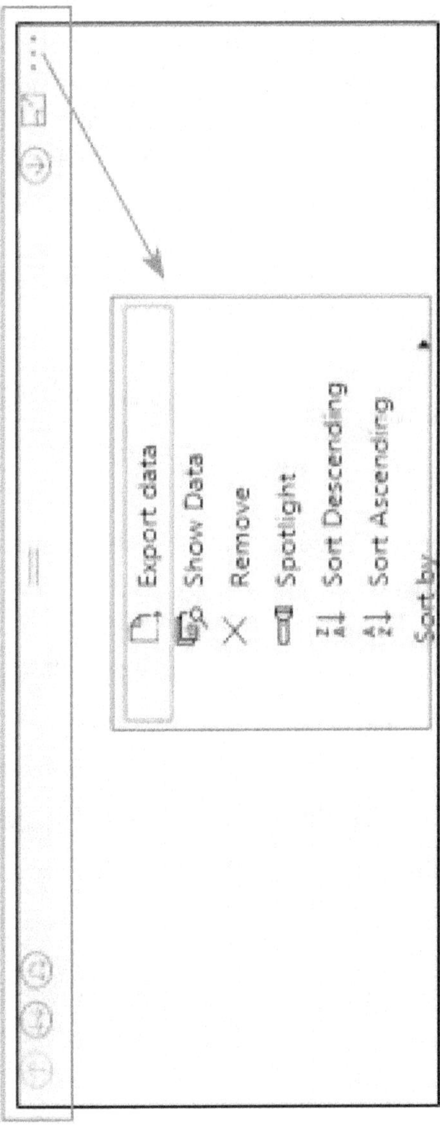

Use filters while creating Power BI reports. With Power BI, you can apply filters to reports to change the data they include based on your requirements.

There are the following kinds of filters available:

A filter at the visual level: Let's say your report has a table, a pie chart, and a bar chart. You would want to filter the data in the bar chart exclusively. In such scenario, you would filter the chart at the visual level.

Page-level filter: You may choose to apply a filter to only one of the ten pages in your report. You could use a page-level filter in that scenario.

Filtering at the report level: A report-level filter is used to apply a filter to your whole report.

Drill-through filter: Similar to how you would dive into data in a graphic, this filter allows you to do the same with data in a report. Let's say, for instance, that your report has a table. To do a more thorough analysis of a particular piece of data in that table, you may use the drill-through filter. You only need to click the Back button to go back to the table.

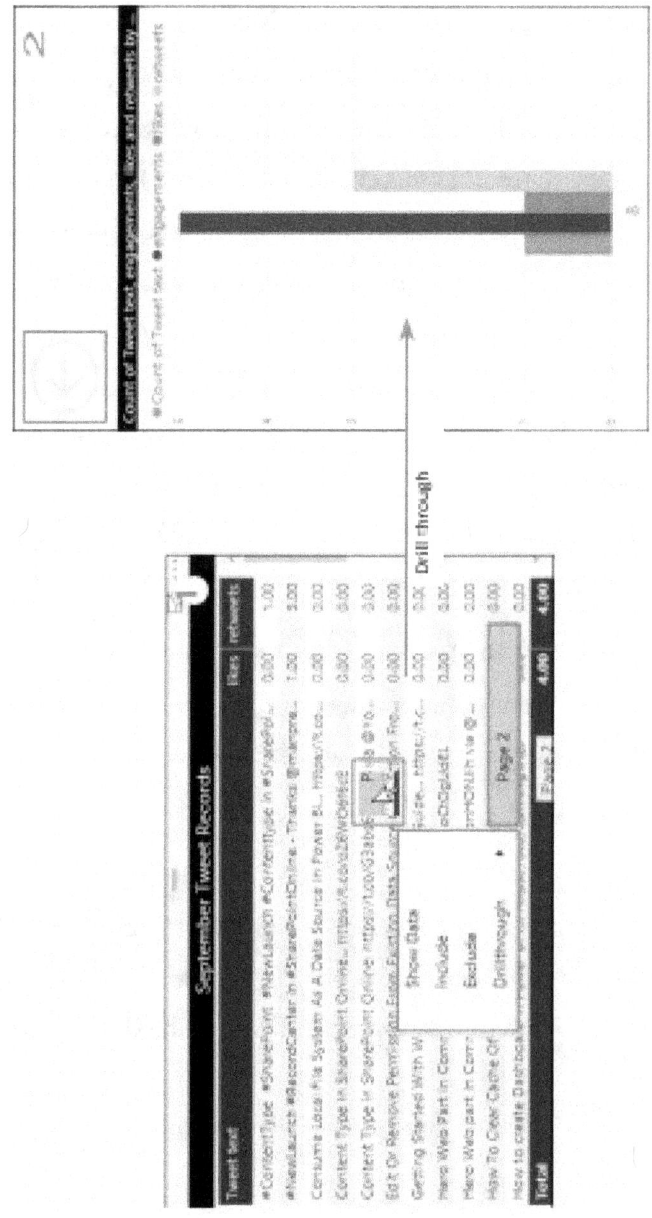
September Tweet Records
Drill through
Show Data
Include
Exclude
Page 2
Total

CHAPTER FOUR

CREATION OF POWER BI REPORTS

The main components of Power BI report development are covered in detail in this chapter, along with techniques and approaches for producing Power BI reports. You will first examine the various data sources that Power BI Desktop and Power BI service offer. After that, you will create an IT cost analysis report using Power BI Desktop. To do this, a data model must be created, data linkages must be established, images must be chosen, and the report must be formatted for both regular and mobile reading. At last, the report will be published.

POWER BI-SUPPORTED DATA SOURCES

You may connect to a variety of data sources using Power BI. The data sources that Power BI Desktop offers are listed in this section.

Sources of data in Power BI Desktop: Multiple data sources are supported by Power BI Desktop. Open Power BI Desktop's File menu, then click Get Data to view and choose from the various data sources. It displays the Get Data page.

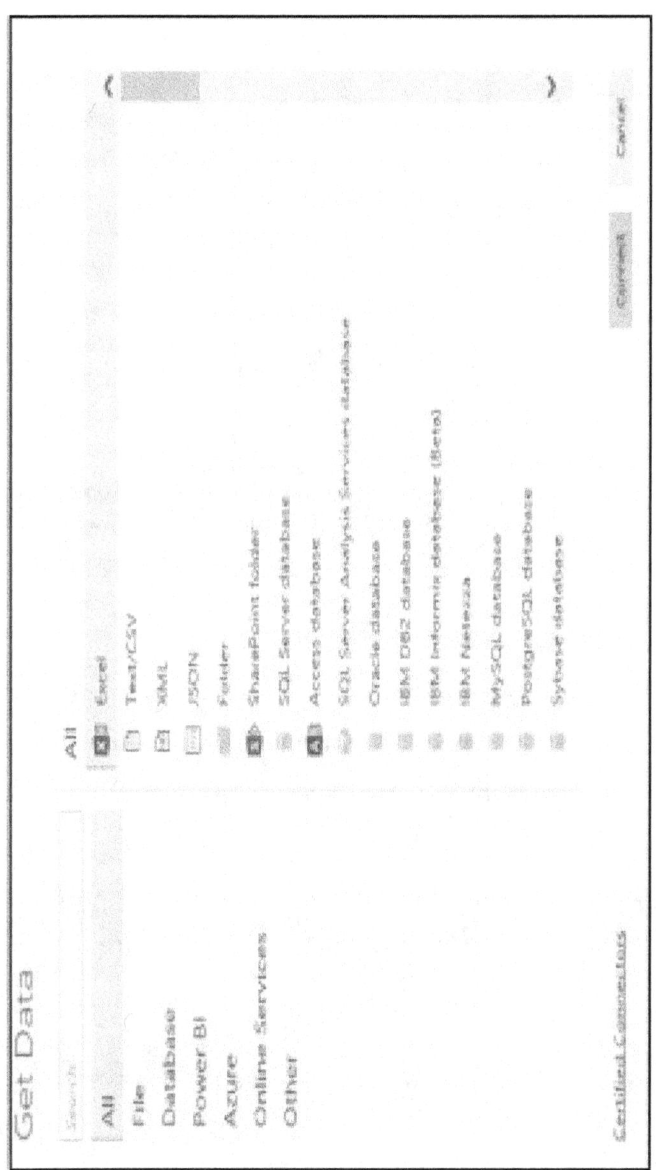
Get Data
All
File
Database
Power BI
Azure
Online Services
Other
Certified Connectors
All
Excel
Text/CSV
XML
JSON
Folder
SharePoint folder
SQL Server database
Access database
SQL Server Analysis Services database
Oracle database
IBM DB2 database
IBM Informix database (Beta)
IBM Netezza
MySQL database
PostgreSQL database
Sybase database
Connect
Cancel

THE POWER BI SERVICE'S DATA SOURCES

The Power BI service divides its data sources into two primary groups:

- To view this page, choose the Get Data option at the bottom of the page after logging into Power BI service.
- AppSource Software Content packs made and shared by other users in your company are included in this category.
- Online services, or third-party services that provide content packs, are also included. (Pre-made data and report collections are called content packs.)

CONNECT TO OR IMPORT DATA

This category includes CSV, XML, and TXT files in addition to Excel workbooks (XLSX and XLXM) and Power BI Desktop files (PBIX). Additionally, it includes database data that is either on-site or on the cloud. Azure SQL Database, Azure SQL Data Warehouse, Azure HDInsight Spark, SQL Server with DirectQuery, and other databases are supported.

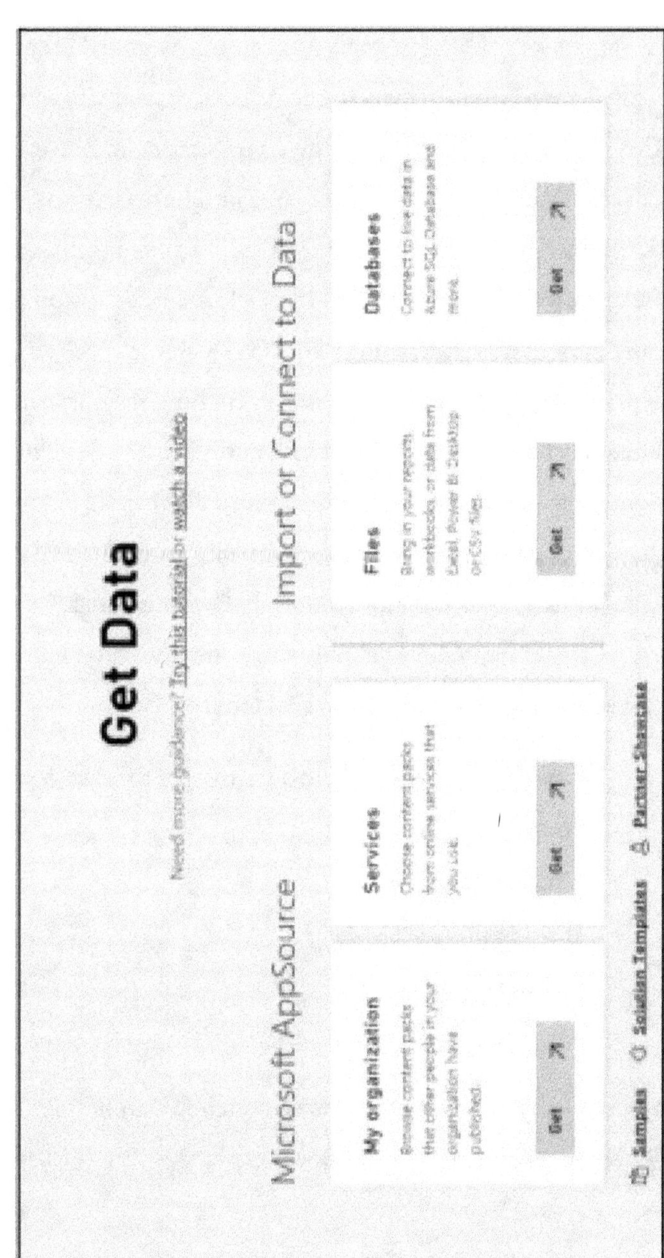
Get Data
Need more guidance? Try this tutorial or watch a video
Microsoft AppSource
Import or Connect to Data
My organization
Get
Services
Get
Files
Get
Databases
Get
Samples
Solution Templates
Partner Showcase

Using Power BI Desktop, create a Power BI report. A great approach to display user data is via Power BI reports. The process for creating a Power BI report in Power BI Desktop is covered in this section. The Microsoft-provided IT Spend Analysis Sample file will serve as the foundation for the report in this part. This file includes information that compares the actual and projected expenses of an IT department. This information aids in creating the company's strategies for the fourth year and identifying any deviations from them. To better assess changes in IT spending during the fiscal year, the organization in this example uses an annual planning cycle but updates its "latest estimate" (LE) every three months. The following are the fundamental procedures for creating a Power BI report:

- Choose the source of the data and get the data model ready.
- Create connections.
- Include images.
- Get the report ready.
- Make the report mobile-friendly.

You publish the report once you've completed all of that. The "Publish the report" section explains this process.

Choose the data source and get the data model ready. You import the data and put it into Power BI Desktop to get the data model ready. The IT Spend Analysis Sample Excel file will be imported in this example.

Take these actions:

- In Power BI Desktop, select the Home tab.
- Choose the Excel option after clicking Get Data.
- Find the IT Spend Analysis Sample file and choose it.
- The tables in the chosen file are shown in the Navigator page of Power BI Desktop. Click the Load button after selecting the checkmark next to each image you wish to use in the Display Options pane.
- The tables are loaded by Power BI. You might need to click the Data View button in order to see them in list form.

- Click the Load button after choosing the tables you wish to include in the data model in Data view.

BUILD CONNECTIONS

Power BI Desktop automatically determines the relationships between tables as you input data. Relationships between tables can also be explicitly set. This section demonstrates how to change and remove connections, activate relationship auto-detection, and manually establish new relationships.

HOW TO CONFIGURE AUTO-DETECT

When you put tables into Power BI Desktop, it automatically determines their relationships. An auto-detect procedure can also be performed manually. Here's how:

- Select the tab for "Home."
- Press the Manage Relationships button
- Click the Autodetect button on the Manage Relationships page

HOW TO MAKE A NEW CONNECTION BY HAND

Use these procedures to manually establish a new relationship:

- Select Manage Relationships from the Home tab.

- Click the New button on the Manage Relationships page.
- The page to create a relationship appears.
- Choose the first table you wish to add to the connection by opening the top drop-down list. Next, decide which column you wish to use as the foundation for the relationship.
- For the bottom drop-down list, repeat step 3 again.
- Press the OK icon.

MODIFY A RELATIONSHIP

You may discover that you need to modify the relationship between two tables after you begin creating your report. Here's how:

- Select Manage Relationships from the Home tab.
- Click the Edit button after checking the box next to the relationship you wish to change on the Manage Relationships page.
- It opens the Edit Relationship page. It resembles the Create Relationship page quite a bit.
- Choose a different table from the top or bottom drop-down list to establish it for the relationship. Alternately, decide to base the relationship on a different column.

- Press the OK icon.

DELETE A RELATIONSHIP

To delete a relationship, follow these steps:

- Select Manage Relationships from the Home tab.
- In the Manage Relationships page, choose the checkbox next to the relationship you wish to eliminate.
- Press the Delete icon.
- The dialog box to delete a relationship opens. Click the Delete button to confirm the deletion

HOW TO INCLUDE IMAGES

You have created relationships and prepared the data model. You are now prepared to include images. Take these actions:

- In Report view, open the report to which you wish to add images.
- Select a visual from the Visualizations window, such as the stacked column chart visual in this case.
- The report page will display a blank image. This is a result of the visual's field parameters not being set.
- At the same time, attributes for the selected visual will display in the Visualizations window.

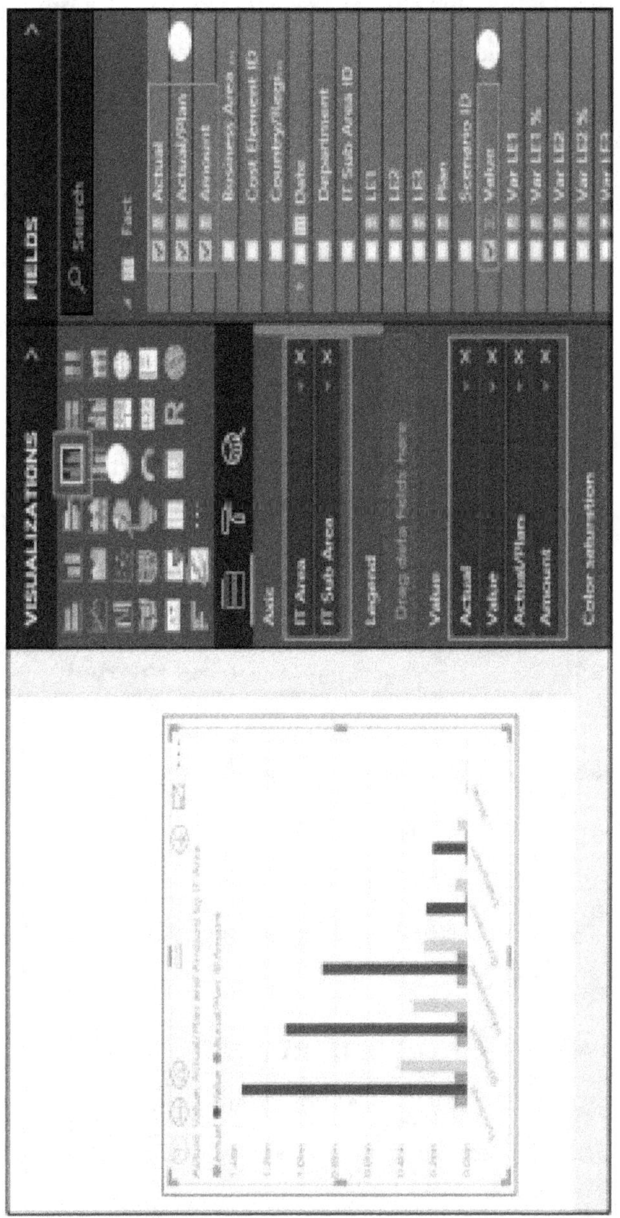

- Select a field you wish to include in the visual in the

Fields pane (in this example, the IT Area field) and drag it to one of the visual's parameters in the Visualizations pane (here, the Axis property).

- To add the IT Sub Area field to the Axis property, repeat step above
- To add the Actual, Value, Actual/Plan, and Amount fields to the Value property, repeat again.
- Get the report ready.
- To compare the Var LE1% and Var LE2% values by cost element group, include a line chart.
- Use a clustered column chart to compare the Actual Sales, Actual/Plan, Amount, and Value data by IT area.
- Display the Var Plan% and Var LE3% figures by nation and sales region using a map graphic.
- Include a bar chart that contrasts the Var Plan% value by business and IT areas.
- To display the Var Plan, Var Plan%, and Actual Sales by business region and time period, use a scatter chart.

HOW TO PREPARE THE REPORT

You may format graphics once you've included them to a report. This part covers the typical formatting choices for a clustered column chart, such as the one made using the data from the IT Spend Analysis Sample file in the previous section. Take the following actions to access these options:

- To choose the image you wish to format in the report, click on it.
- Click the Format icon (which has a paint roller) at the bottom of the Visualizations window.
- A formatting category list is displayed.
- Click the down arrow next to the category name to see the choices under that category.
- A toggle to enable or disable the options in a certain category is a characteristic of several categories.
- Click on a category's toggle to make it active or inactive.

HOW TO MAKE THE REPORT MOBILE-FRIENDLY

- With Power BI Desktop, you can use the Power BI mobile application—available for Windows, iOS, and Android devices—to optimize your report for mobile consumption.
- Open the IT Spend Analysis Report 02-Formatted.pbix example report in Power BI Desktop.

Then do the following actions to make it mobile-friendly:

- Select the View tab in the Report window, then select the Phone Layout button. A mobile device-shaped blank canvas appears.
- Drag a graphic to the empty canvas after clicking on it in the Visualizations.
- Continue until the mobile canvas displays every required image.
- Adjust the images' size and placement as needed.
- Click the View tab and select Desktop Layout to return to Desktop view.

One of the following actions can be used to delete a visual from the mobile canvas:

- Click the X button in the upper-right corner of the mobile canvas's image when in Phone Layout view.
- Pick the image from the mobile canvas and hit the keyboard's Delete key.

HOW TO UPLOAD YOUR REPORT TO THE POWER BI PLATFORM

You may publish your report to the Power BI service as a last step once you have finished formatting and preparing it. A report that has been published to the Power BI service is accessible from the cloud by others.

Use these procedures to publish a report from Power BI Desktop to Power BI service:

- Select the File option.
- Select "Publish to Power BI."
- Another option is to choose the Home tab and then click the Publish button.
- Enter your Power BI login information when required.
- The page to publish to Power BI appears.
- Click the Select button after choosing the workspace—in this example, My Workspace—on which you wish to publish the report.
- A dialog window for progress appears. Once the process is finished, a success message will appear.
- Click "Publish."

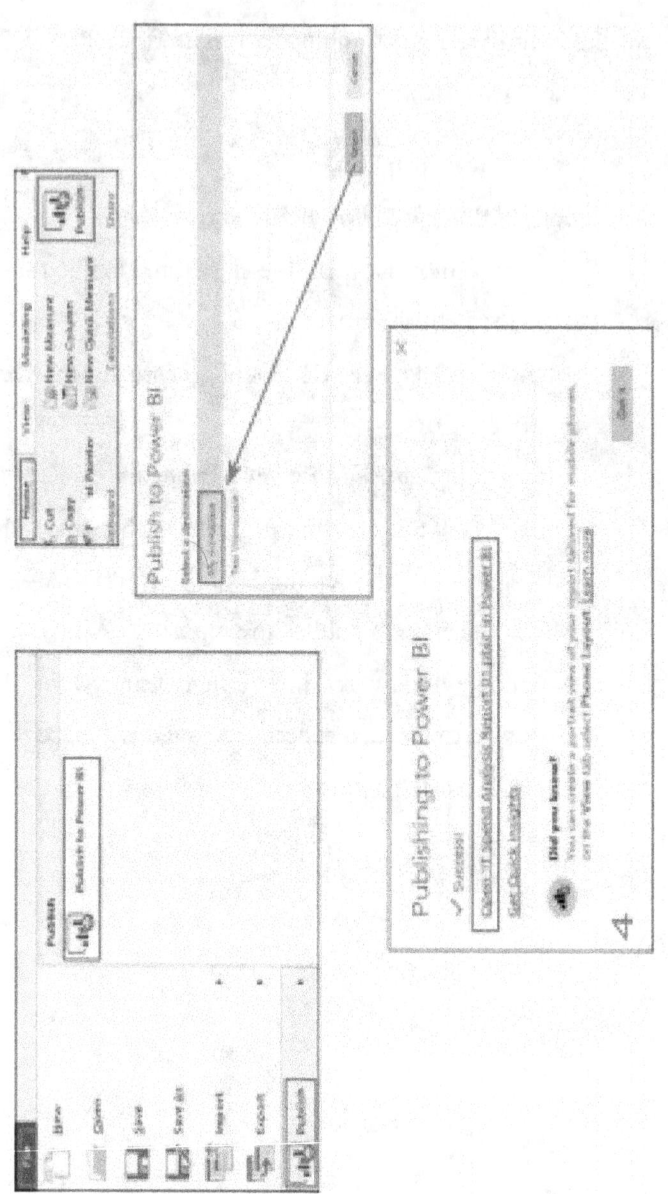
Publish to Power BI
Publishing to Power BI

HOW TO UTILIZE DAX WITH POWER BI

A set of functions, operators, and constants known as Data Analysis Expressions (DAX) are used to handle simple data computations in order to improve data analysis and address business issues. You may create or implement functions in Power BI that make use of pre-existing data by using DAX. Assume, for instance, that you wish to include a column that computes sales growth as a % in a Power BI report that contains data on product sales. This may be accomplished with DAX with ease.

There are two words you should be familiar with before diving into DAX:

- **The Calculated column**: Data from two existing columns may be calculated using DAX, and the outcome is shown in a new column. We refer to this new column as **a Calculated column**.
- **Assess**: As you work with your Power BI reports, such as by adding filters and other actions, a measure dynamically calculates your data and refreshes the results in real time.

Two categories of measurements exist:

- **Easy steps:** These are basic data computations. The total of an organization's sales is an illustration of a basic metric.
- **Complicated procedures**: These are computations that integrate two or more data tables or include extra filters.

HOW TO CREATE A CALCULATED COLUMN IN POWER BI

- Go to Data view in Power BI to create a calculated column.

Next, take one of the actions listed below:

- Click the New Column button in the Calculations group under the Modeling tab.
- Right-click on the table name and choose New Column from the menu that shows up.
- A box allowing you to enter the necessary calculation in DAX form appears when you create the new column.
- Once the computation has been entered, click the checkbox to the left of the box or press Enter.
- Assume, for instance, that the table includes the amount sold and the number of units per price. The entire sales amount may then be displayed by

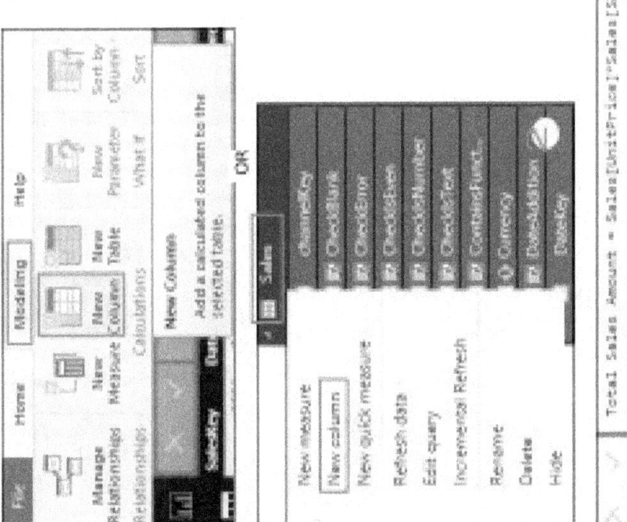

combining these two pieces of data in the computed

column.

For usage in your computations, you can define variables for a variety of functions.

vPrice: The sales value per unit price is represented by this variable.

Quantity: This variable relates to the volume of sales. The entire sales amount is calculated in the RETURN function by multiplying vPrice by vQuantity.

HOW TO MAKE A POWER BI MEASURE

You have two options for creating a new measure from the Data view, much like with calculated columns: Click the New Measure button in the Calculations group under the Modeling tab.

- Choose New Measure from the menu that displays when you right-click the table name.
- Once more, a box allowing you to add the necessary function or expression in DAX form appears after you create the measure.
- Once you have done so, click the checkbox to the left of the box or hit Enter.

For instance, let's say you wish to find sales patterns using sales data. The following statement, which aggregates total sales, might be used to generate a new measure (Sales Measure).

Sales [Total Sales Amount] = sum(Sales) is the sales measure.

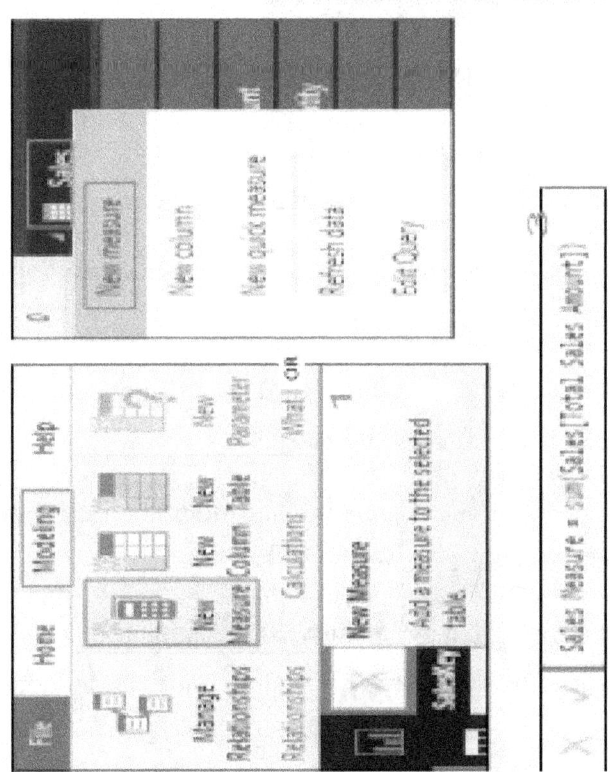

Take prompt action.

Microsoft offers a number of pre-defined measurements that you may choose from in addition to creating your own using DAX. These predetermined measurements, often known as fast measures, may be found online.

The following categories comprise quick measures: Filters, Aggregate Within a Category, and Time Intelligence

- Text
- Total
- Mathematical Operations

In a category, **aggregate Average for each category**: This determines the category-wide average of the base value.

Variance by category: This determines the base value's variation within the category.

Maximum for each category: This determines the base value's maximum inside the category.

Minimum for each category: This determines the lowest base value in the category.

Average weighted by category: This determines a weighted average of each category's base value. You divide by the sum of the weights after multiplying the value by the weight of each category.

FUNCTION OF QUICK MEASURE

FILTERS

Value that has been filtered: This applies a filter and computes a value.

Variation from the filtered value: This determines how much a value differs from its value after a filter has been applied.

Percentage of the filtered value that differs: This determines how much a value differs from its value after a filter has been applied.

New category sales: Sales from clients making their first purchase are calculated in this way. This metric may also be used to determine the average age of clients paying for life insurance, the number of people calling the support desk for the first time, and other information.

INTELLIGENCE IN TIME

Total for the year thus far: This determines the base value's total from the start of the current year.

Total for the current quarter: This determines the base value's total from the start of the current quarter.

Total for the month: This determines the base value's total from the start of the current month.

Change from year to year: This determines the base value's change from year to year.

Change from quarter to quarter: This determines the base value's change from quarter to quarter.

Change from month to month: This determines the base value's change from month to month.

The rolling average: This determines the base value's average over a predetermined number of periods prior to and/or following each date.

TOTALS

Running total: This determines a measure's running total in a particular field.

Total for category (filters applied): Using the filters in your report, this determines the sum of all the values in a category.

Total for category (filters not applied): This determines the sum of all the values in a category without taking into account any filters that may have been used in your report.

OPERATIONS IN MATHEMATICS

- **Moreover**: The sum of two values is computed in this way.
- **Deduction**: This determines how much two values differ from one another.
- **The act of multiplying**: The product of two values is computed in this way.
- **Separation**: This determines a value's ratio to another.
- **The percentage difference:** This determines the two values' percentage difference.
- **Coefficient of correlation:** The correlation coefficient between two values in a category is computed in this way.
- **Text Star Rating:** This creates a changeable star rating from a numeric number.
- **Concatenated values in a list:** This results in a list of unique values in a column that are separated by commas.

Let's say you want to examine the total sales for each product category separately, year-to-date, and you have a report that shows the overall sales amount for all product categories.

Because this kind of data is changing, a rapid measure must be used. To make one, follow these steps:

- Select the New Quick Measure button from the Home menu.
- You may also choose New fast Measure by right-clicking the table for which you wish to create a new fast measure.
- The dialog window for Quick Measures appears.
- All of the quick measure function's parameters are listed on the left side of the dialog box, and the fields that are available inside the function that has been selected are listed on the right.
- Click on Calculation and choose Average Per Category.
- Select the Sum of Sales Amount option from the Base Value drop-down menu.
- Select Product Key from the Category drop-down menu.
- To use the fast measure, click OK. To see a formula bar with the quick measure's DAX code, double-click the measure's name.

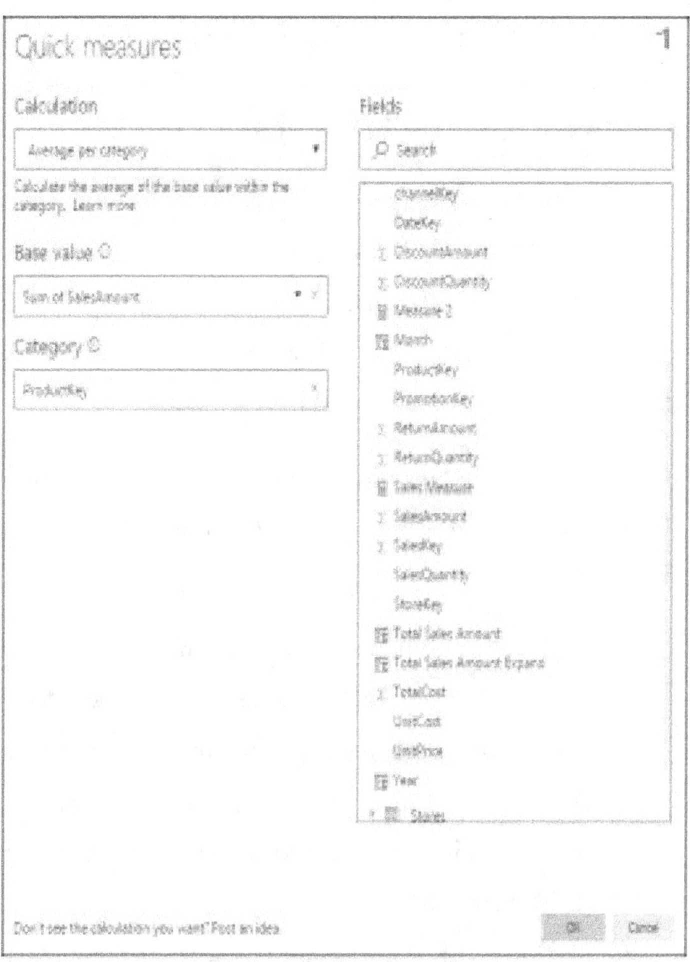


```
SalesAmount average per ProductKey 2 =
AVERAGEX(
    KEEPFILTERS(VALUES('Sales'[ProductKey])),
    CALCULATE(SUM('Sales'[SalesAmount]))
)
```

2

The syntax and context of DAX expressions
As you now know, you may evaluate important data for Power BI reports using DAX expressions. The syntax and context of these phrases are particular.

DAX EXPRESSION SYNTAX

As previously stated, DAX expressions follow a certain syntax. To determine the total sales from a table of sales data, for instance, use the following DAX expression:
Total Sales (Sales[Price]) = SUM

The following components are present in this expression:
Total Sales This is the computed column's or measure's name.

- = This operator indicates that the function has begun. SUMMARY All of the values in the Sales[Price] column are added together using this DAX function.
- () At least one argument is enclosed in parenthesis. Sales This is a reference to the table's name that is being examined.
- The cost The SUM function will be applied to this column in the table.

DAX EXPRESSION CONTEXT

You need to take context into account while doing complicated dynamic analysis. The data that may be used to accomplish a computation is referred to as context. Two contexts are supported by DAX expressions:

- **The context of Row**: When a function in a DAX formula uses filters to identify a single row in a table, row context is applicable. Stated otherwise, the computation is limited to a single row. Generally speaking, it has to employ specific methods correctly in order to reference any data that is outside of that row. Instead of being determined at run time, the row context is determined during processing. When creating computed columns, this kind of context is helpful.
- **Contextual filtering:** The use of one or more filters in a computation to arrive at a certain value or result is referred to as filter context. Row context is extended by filter context, not replaced. To apply a filter context, you utilize the DAX methods listed below:
- Associated
- Filter
- Compute

An illustration of a computation using row context is provided. and Category are the two tables that are displayed in Power BI Desktop. A new computed column is also displayed.

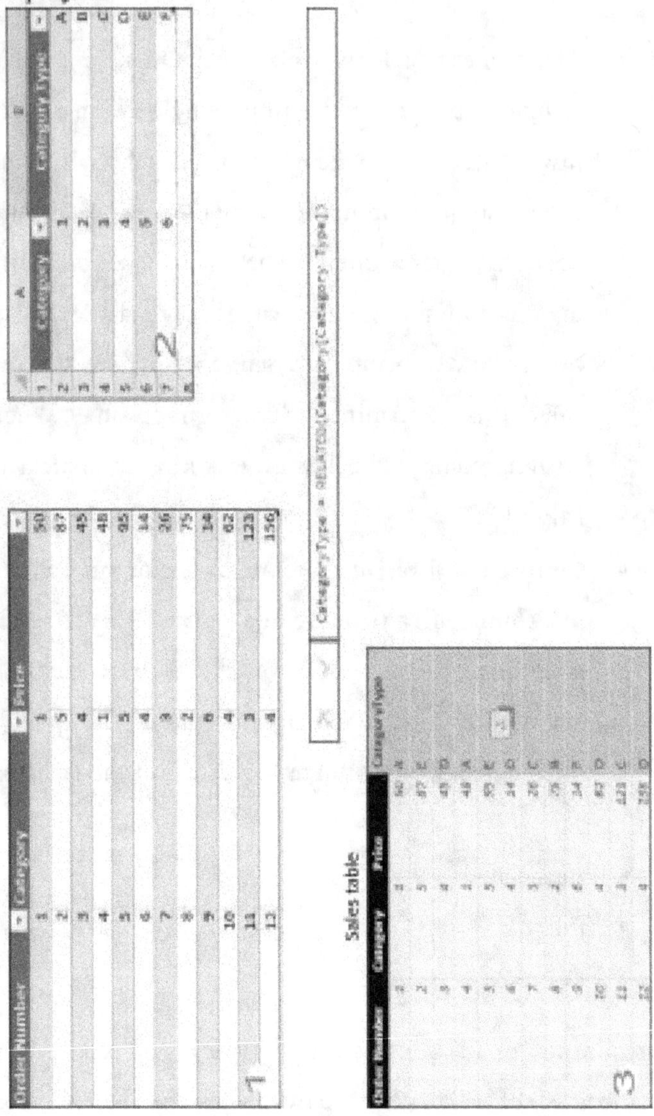

Keep in mind that the relationship between the two tables does not affect the row context. I used the RELATED DAX expression to do Category[Category Type] = RELATED(Category)

As a result, the filter context was created from the row context. (We refer to this process as context shifting.)

The data in a table is calculated by DAX functions. Different kinds of DAX functions exist, including:

Time intelligence functions, date and time functions, filter functions, information functions, and **logical functions.**
Functions related to math and parents and children Text functions, statistical functions, and other functions.

Time and date functions: Expressions involving dates and times make use of these functions.

The following are the functions:

- **CALENDAR**:

When you give a start date and an end date, this method produces a sequence of dates. (The method produces an error if the start date is later than the end date.) It employs the syntax shown below:

CALENDAR(<start_date>, <end_date>)

- **DATE:**

A particular date is returned by this method. The syntax it used is:

DATE(<year>, <month>, <day>)

The following formula, for instance, yields a date in the format of year-month-date: DATE(2025,6,11) is in column

- **DATEDIFF:**

An interval count between two given dates is returned by this method. (The method produces an error if the start date is later than the end date.) It employs the syntax shown below:

DATEDIFF(<start_date>, <end_date>, <interval>)

The following phrase, for instance, yields the difference in minutes between two dates:

DATEDIFF('Table'[Date],'Table'[Column],MINUTE) is the Date Difference.

- **NOW:**

The current time and date are returned by this function. The formula will compute the value using all of the column data if you choose to show this information in a calculated column. It employs the syntax shown below:

NOW()

- **WEEKDAY**:

This indicates the fifth day of the week by returning a number between 0 and 6 or between 1 and 7. You indicate the day each number corresponds to.

Here are a few typical trends:

In Pattern 1, Sunday is represented by the number 0, Monday by the number 1, Tuesday by the number 2, Wednesday by the number 3, and so on.

Pattern 2: If the number 1 corresponds to Sunday, then the number 2 corresponds to Monday, the number 3 to Tuesday, the number 4 to Wednesday, and so on.

Pattern 3: If the number 1 corresponds to Monday, then the number 2 corresponds to Tuesday, the number 3 to Wednesday, the number 4 to Thursday, and so on.

The syntax used by this function is as follows:

WEEKDAY(<date>, <return_type>)

For instance, the DAX statement that follows takes a date-time field and returns a weekday: WEEKDAY('Table'[Date],2) = WeekDay

TODAY: The current time and date are returned by this function. It employs the syntax shown below: TODAY(<date>)

THE YEAR: The current year is returned by this method. It employs the syntax shown below:

YEAR(<date>)

- **TIME**:

This changes the hour-minute-second format of a time value to the one used for computed columns. To make tables easier to read, this is advised.

The syntax it used is TIME(<hour>, <minute>, <second>)

FUNCTIONS OF TIME INTELLIGENCE

For instance, these routines provide data for sales inventories and other computations using calendar data. Among them are the following:

- **DATEADD**:

Starting with a given date, this function adds (or subtracts) a predetermined number of years, quarters, months, or days, and then returns the result. It employs the syntax shown below:

DATEADD(<date>, <number_of_intervals>, <interval>)

For instance, the following DAX expression might be used to add a one-month interval to dates that are shown in a DateKey column in a Calendar table:

('Calendar'[DateKey],1,MONTH) = DateAddition

- **DATESMTD**:

A list of dates from the beginning of the month to the present day, arranged chronologically, is returned by this month-to-date function.

It employs the syntax shown below:

DATESMTD(<dates>)

where the column with the pertinent dates is denoted by <dates>.

- **DATESQTD**:

The dates from the beginning of the quarter to the present day are returned chronologically by this quarter-to-date function. It employs the syntax shown below: DATESQTD(<dates>)

- **DATESYTD**:

A chronological list of dates from the beginning of the year to the present is returned by this year-to-date function. It employs the syntax shown below:

DATESYTD(<dates> [,<year_end_date>])

where the current day of the year is denoted by <year_end_date>.

- **TOTALMTD**:

This function computes a value and displays, month-by-month, the data that was utilized to get that result. It employs the syntax shown below:

TOTALMTD(<expression>, <dates>[, <filter>])

Let's say, for instance, that you wish to figure up total sales and arrange them by month. The following phrase might be used in the situation:

'Sales'[Sales] + 'Dates'[Dates] = TOTALMTD

- **TOTALQTD**:

Although it arranges the data according to quarters, this function is the same as TOTALMTD.

It employs the syntax shown below:

TOTALQTD(<expression>, <dates>[, <filter>])

- **TOTALYTD**: Similar to TOTALMTD and TOTALQTD, this function arranges the data according to the current year. It employs the syntax shown below:

TOTALYTD(<expression>, <dates>[, <filter>][, <year_end_date>]

FUNCTIONS FOR FILTERS

These routines return a subset of an expression after filtering data using commands. With the use of tables and connections, they enable intricate dynamic computations. Among them are the following:

- **FILTER**:

When necessary, this method returns an expression or a subset of a table after filtering data from the table. It employs the syntax shown below:

FILTER(<table>, <filter>)

Let's say, for instance, that you wish to see all sales information for goods that cost more than $120. You might use the FILTER function in the manner shown below to do this:

COUNTROWS(FILTER('Sales', 'Sales' [Sales] > 120)) = FilterSample

A selection of rows with sales values higher than 120 will be the end result.

- **RELATED:**

Relationships between values in several tables are found using this function. It employs the syntax shown below: RELATED(<column>)

Let's say, for instance, that you wish to obtain US sales information from many tables. The following phrase would be used by you:

COUNTROWS(FILTER(ALL('Sales'), RELATED('SalesGeography' [Countries]) = "United States") is the RelatedSample.

- **ALL:**

Regardless of any filters used, this method returns every value in a table or column. It employs the syntax shown below:

ALL(<table> or <column>)

Consider counting every row of sales data regardless of any page-level filters that are in place as an illustration of the

ALL function. In this situation, the phrase is: COUNTROWS(ALL('Sales')) = ALL Sales Order

Because the filters are disregarded in this expression, users can use the ALL function to retrieve the complete count of data collected.

- CALCULATE:

Among the most crucial DAX functions is this one. This determines an expression's value while applying filters. It employs the syntax shown below:

CALCULATE(<expression>, <filter1>, <filter2> ….)For instance, you might use the following formula to get the total sales at every location:

CALCULATE(SUM('Sales'[Sales]),ALL('SalesGeography') = CalculateSample

FUNCTIONS OF INFORMATION

These functions, which comprise the following, give details about the cell or row that has been detected in a query:

- **CONTAINS**:

If the value or text you are looking for does indeed occur in the designated column or row, this method returns TRUE; if not, it returns FALSE.

It employs the syntax shown below:

CONTAINS (<table>. <columnName>, <value>[, <columnName>, <value>]….)

- **ISBLANK**:

This function determines if a table cell is blank. It returns TRUE if it is the case, and FALSE otherwise.

It employs the syntax shown below:

ISBLANK(<value>)

- **ISERROR**:

This function determines if a string or value includes an error. It returns FALSE otherwise; if so, it returns TRUE.

It employs the syntax shown below:

ISERROR (<value>)

- **ISTEXT**:

This function determines if a given value is text. It returns FALSE otherwise; if so, it returns TRUE.

It employs the syntax shown below:

ISTEXT (<value>)

- **ISNUMBER**:

This function determines if a given value is a number or not. It returns FALSE otherwise; if so, it returns TRUE.

It employs the syntax shown below:

ISNUMBER (<number>)

- **ISEVEN**:

This function determines if a given number is even. It returns TRUE if it is the case, and FALSE if it is not, signifying that the number is odd.

It employs the syntax shown below:

ISEVEN (<number>)

CHAPTER FIVE

FUNCTIONS OF LOGIC

You may add decision-making skills to your DAX expressions by using logical functions. Among these are the following functions:

- **IF**:

This function verifies a statement's condition. The function runs one parameter if the condition is TRUE. The function runs a different argument (or no argument at all) if it is FALSE.

It employs the syntax shown below:

IF(<logical_test>, <value_if_true>, <value_if_false>)

The parameters of this expression are as follows:

Let's say, for instance, that you wish to find large orders (more than 150 units). You might use the following phrase to do this:

IF(Sales[Sales]>150,"Large Order","Small Order") = CheckLargeOrder

- **AND**

Several criteria are checked by this function. It returns TRUE if every condition is TRUE. If not, FALSE is returned.

AND(<logic1>, <logic2>)

<logic1>, <logic2> Are conditions to be checked

Let's say, for instance, that you wish to find all large orders (more than 150 units) in a certain nation (whose country ID is 5). You might use the following phrase to do this:

If, checkLargewithAND("Correct","In Correct") (AND(Sales[Sales]>150,Sales[CountryID]=5)

- **OR**:

Several criteria are checked by this function. The function returns TRUE if any one of the conditions is TRUE. If not, FALSE is returned.

It employs the syntax shown below: OR(<logic1>, <logic2>)

Let's say, for instance, that you wish to find all orders in a certain nation (whose country ID is 5) or large orders (more than 150 units). The following phrase might be used in the CheckLargewithOR =

IF(OR(Sales[Sales]>150,Sales[CountryID]=5),"Correct", "In Correct")

- **SWITCH**:

You can change one value for another with this function. It employs the syntax shown below:

SWITCH(<expression>, <value>, <result>[, <value>, <result>]…[, <else>])

Assume, for instance, that you wish to replace the month names with the month numbers. This is accomplished via the following expression:

MonthName = SWITCH(Dates[Month], 1, "January", 2, "February", 3, "March", 4,

"April", 5, "May", 6, "June", 7, "July", 8, "August", 9, "September", 10, "October", 11, "November", 12, "December", "Unknown month number")

FUNCTIONS IN MATHEMATICS

You can do mathematical computations on your data by using math functions. Among these are the following functions:

- **SUM**:

All of the values in a specified column are added using this function. It employs the syntax shown below:

SUM(<column>)

All of the values for which the sum operation has to be carried out are contained in this column. A decimal number is the value that was returned.

- **SUMX**:

Although it applies criteria to the rows and columns in a whole table and calculates row-by-row, this function is comparable to the SUM function. The syntax it use is SUMX(<table>, <expression>)

- **FACT**:

A given number's factorial is returned by this function. It employs the five syntaxes listed below:

FACT(<number>)

- **GCD**

For two or more integers, this function yields the greatest common divisor (without a remainder). It employs the syntax shown below:

GCD(number1, [number2], ….)

For instance, the greatest common divisor (4) for the numbers 4 and 12 may be obtained using the following expression:
GCD(4, 12) = GCDValue

A #VALUE! error is returned by GCD if any of the values it finds are not numeric. A #NUM! error is returned by GCD if any of the values are less than zero.

- **LCM:**

For two or more numbers, the function yields the least common multiple. It employs the syntax shown below:

LCM(number1, [number2], ...)

- **POWER:**

This function gives back, in decimal form, the value of an integer raised to a certain power. It employs the syntax shown below:

POWER(<number>, <power>)

For instance, the value of 5 increased by a power of 2 is 25, which is the result of the following statement.
POWER = POWER(5,2)

- **ROUND:**

The value of an integer rounded to the closest decimal place is returned by this function. It employs the syntax shown below:

ROUND(<number>, <num_digit>)

FUNCTIONS OF PARENT AND CHILD

The parent/child hierarchy may be managed using a variety of DAX methods. The parent in the current row hierarchy, the descendant n levels from the top of the current row hierarchy, the number of levels to the top parent, the parent n levels above the current row, and the full lineage of parents of a row may all be obtained using these functions. Among these are the following functions:

- **PATH**:

You may use this method to find the parents of the chosen child value.

It employs the syntax shown below:
PATH(<ID_columnName>, <parent_columnName>)

- **PATHITEM**:

A delimited string with parent nodes is the output of the PATH function. The PATHITEM function is used to return a specific item that was retrieved by the PATH function, depending on where the item is located in the results (from top to bottom or left to right). It employs the syntax shown below:

PATHITEM(<path>, <position>[, <type>])

- **PATHLENGTH**

The number of parents between two provided objects is returned by this function. It employs the syntax shown below:

PATHLENGTH(<path>)

- **PATHITEMREVERSE**:

This function is PATHITEM's opposite. From bottom to top or right to left, it returns a specific item in the PATH results. It employs the syntax shown below:

PATHITEMREVERSE(<path>, <position>[, <type>])

FUNCTIONS OF STATISTICS

These functions handle sums, averages, and aggregations of the numbers in a column. These consist of the following:

- **AVERAGE**:

The average of every number in a column is determined by this function. It employs the syntax listed below: AVERAGE(<column>)

- **COUNT**:

This function determines how many cells in a given column contain numbers overall. It employs the syntax listed below: COUNT(<column>)

- **MAX**

The greatest number from a column or between two scalar expressions is returned by this function. It employs the syntax listed below:

MAX(<column>)

MAX(<expression1>, <expression2>)

- **MIN**:

The smallest value from a column or between two scalar expressions is returned by this function. It employs the syntax listed below:

MIN(<column>)

MIN(<expression1>, <expression2>)

FUNCTION OF TEXT

You can perform actions on text in tables and columns by using text functions. Among these are the following functions:

- **CONCATENATE**:

This function creates a single string from two strings of text, integers, or Boolean values. It employs the syntax listed below:

CONCATENATE(<Text1>, <Text2>)

Assume, for instance, that you wish to merge the text strings "Hello" and "World" into a single new string. The following phrase could be used:

CONCATENATE("Hello", "World")

- **REPLACE**

Any portion of a text string can be replaced with a new text string with this function. It employs the syntax listed below:

REPLACE (<old_text>, <start_num>, <num_chars>, <new_text>)

- **TRIM**:

With the exception of single spaces (5 between words), this function eliminates all spaces from a text stream. It employs the syntax listed below:

TRIM(<text>)

- **UPPER**:

All of the letters in a text string are changed to capital letters with this function. It employs the syntax listed below: UPPER (<text>)

ADDITIONAL FUNCTIONS

Two functions that do not fall under any other category are covered in this section:

- **EXCEPT**:

Values that are present in one table but absent from another are returned by this function. (Note that the number of columns in each tables must be equal.) It employs the syntax listed below:

EXCEPT(<table_expression1>, <table_expression2>)

- **UNION**:

A new table made out of certain columns from an existing table is returned by this function. It employs the syntax listed below:

UNION(<table_expression1>, <table_expression2> [, <table_expression>] …)

CHAPTER SIX

CREATE POWER BI REPORTS USING EXCEL

The creation of a Power BI report that uses a Microsoft Excel workbook as its data source will be covered in this chapter. A retail chain's sales will be examined in the report. This chapter is the first of several that will walk you through the process of creating different kinds of reports and importing data from several sources. However, keep in mind that the report formats covered in relation to one data source, like Excel, could also be applied to other data sources, like a list in SharePoint Online. The purpose of this is to help you learn how to create Power BI reports and to support your exploration of the many applications of Power BI.

HOW TO USE POWER BI TO IMPORT DATA FROM AN EXCEL WORKBOOK

Use these procedures to import the data into Power BI Desktop from the Retail Analysis Sample.xlsx Excel workbook:

- In Power BI Desktop, select the Home tab.
- Choose the File option after clicking Get Data.
- Select Connect after clicking Excel Workbook.

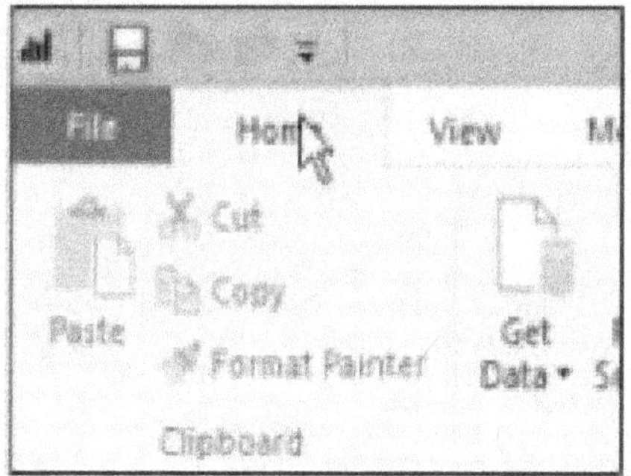
File
View
Paste
Cut
Copy
Format Painter
Clipboard
Get
Data

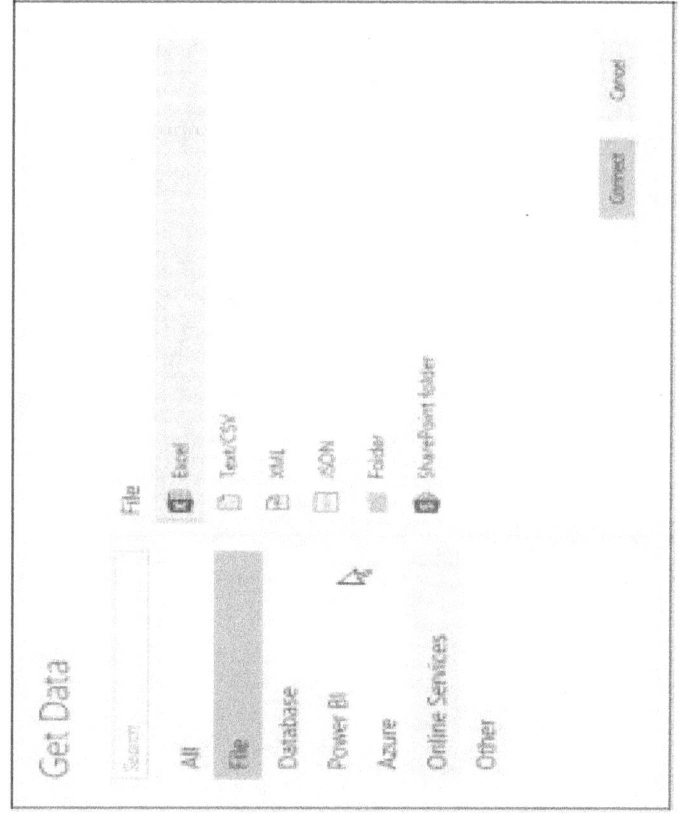
Get Data
All
File
Database
Power BI
Azure
Online Services
Other
File
Excel
Text/CSV
XML
JSON
Folder
SharePoint folder
Connect
Cancel

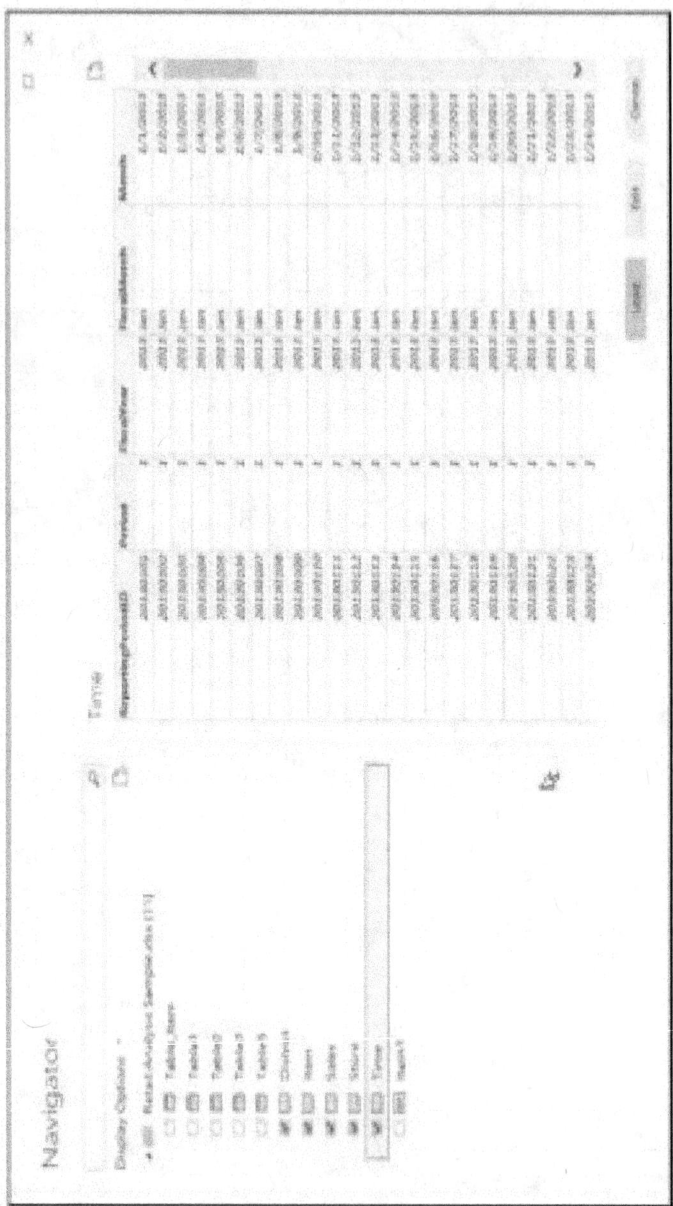
Navigator
Time

Locate and pick the Retail Analysis Sample.xlsx workbook.

- Select the tables (Store table, etc.) you wish to include in your report and click Load.
- To go to Data view, click the Data View button on the left side of the screen.

HOW TO INCLUDE A CALCULATED COLUMN AND A MEASURE

Let's say you want this report to incorporate a calculated column that pulls some more fields from the columns or data you currently have, and a measure that does different calculations based on the sales data.

Use these procedures to add the measure:

- Select the Store table you imported from Excel, then select New Measure under the Modeling menu.

Or

- Use the option that comes when you right-click the Store table and select New Measure.
- In the formula bar, a new measure appears.
- Give the new metric the name Total Stores.
- Enter the desired DAX expression, in this example COUNTA.

- Select the column to which the measure should be applied by clicking the column placeholder; in this example, it is Store([StoreNumberName.
- To finish the formula, click the checkmark in the formula bar or press Enter.

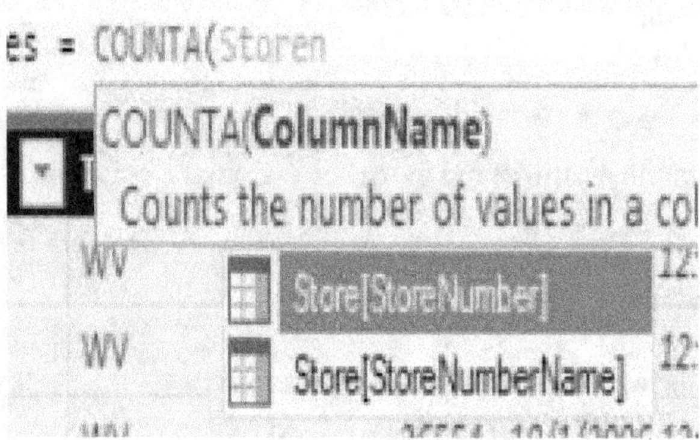

NAMES OF MEASURE AND FORMULA

- **TOTAL UNITS THIS YEAR**

Total Units This Year = CALCULATE([TotalUnits], Sales[ScenarioID]=1)

- **REGULAR_SALES_DOLLARS**

Regular_Sales_Dollars = SUM([Sum_Regular_Sales_Dollars])

- **TOTALSALES**

TotalSales = [Regular_Sales_Dollars]+[Markdown_Sales_Dollars]

- **AVG $/UNIT TY**

Avg $/Unit TY = IF([Total Units This Year]<>0, [TotalSal-esTY]/[Total Units This Year], BLANK())

- **MARKDOWN_SALES_DOLLARS**

Markdown_Sales_Dollars = SUM([Sum_Markdown_Sales_Dollars])

- **TOTALSALESTY**

TotalSalesTY = CALCULATE([TotalSales], Sales[ScenarioID]=1)

- **TOTALUNITS**

TotalUnits = [Regular_Sales_Units]+[Markdown_Sales_Units]

- **REGULAR_SALES_UNITS**

Regular_Sales_Units = SUM([Sum_Regular_Sales_Units])

- **MARKDOWN_SALES_UNITS**

Markdown_Sales_Units = SUM([Sum_Markdown_Sales_Units])

- **TOTAL SALES VARIANCE**

Total Sales Variance = [Total Sales Var]

- **TOTAL SALES VAR**

Total Sales Var = [TotalSalesTY]-[TotalSalesLY]

- **TOTALSALESTY**

TotalSalesTY = CALCULATE([TotalSales], Sales[ScenarioID]=1)

- **TOTALSALESLY**

TotalSalesLY = CALCULATE([TotalSales], Sales[ScenarioID]=2)

- **THIS YEAR SALES**

This Year Sales = [TotalSalesTY]

- **TOTALSALESTY**

TotalSalesTY = CALCULATE([TotalSales], Sales[ScenarioID]=1)

HOW TO GENERATE CALCULATED COLUMN

Take the following actions to generate the calculated column:

- Select the Store table, then select New Column under the Modeling tab.

Or

- Use the option that comes when you right-click the Store table and select New Column.
- The formula bar shows up.
- Give the newly computed column the name Open Month.
- Enter the desired DAX expression, in this example FORMAT.
- Choose the [OpenDate] option.
- Enter parameter indicated.
- After that, include a closing parenthesis.
- To finish the formula, click the checkmark in the formula bar or press Enter.

HOW TO INCLUDE POWER BI VISUAL IN THE REPORT

You may improve your Power BI report with visuals. You will include the following images in this area of your report:

- **The attribute slicer**: To display the total sales value by category, you will utilize an attribute slicer.

- **A multi-row card**: Store information by category will be displayed on a multi-row card.
- **A waterfall chart**: The total unit price by month and category will be displayed in a waterfall chart.
- **A bubble chart**: The total sales variance, the average price per unit this year, and the sales by category for the current year will all be displayed using a bubble chart.
- **A line chart:** The sales for the current year by district manager and category will be displayed on a line graph.

HOW TO ADD ATTRIBUTE SLICER (TOTAL SALES BY CATEGORY)

Include an attribute slicer in the report to display total sales by category. The attribute slicer can be accessed in Power BI's Visualizations pane just like any other visual once you've downloaded and installed it.

You can filter data according to various categories by using an attribute slicer. An attribute slicer that filters data by category and total sales will be added in this scenario.

- Open the Visualizations pane and expand the attribute slicer options.

- Drag the Category field to the Items item in the attribute slicer settings after selecting it in the Fields pane to the right of the Visualizations pane.
- Drag the With Values entry to the TotalSales field.

HOW TO ADD A MULTI-ROW CARD

You will add a multi-row card to show store details by category. Take these actions:

- Open the Visualizations pane and expand the multi-row card options.
- Drag the Chain field to the Fields item in the multi-row card settings after selecting it in the Fields pane to the right of the Visualizations pane.
- Move the Name and Chain fields below each other.
- Move the Category space beneath the Name space.
- Move the Category field beneath the Avg $/Unit TY field.

HOW TO ADD A WATERFALL CHART

You can display time-based data with ongoing computations using a waterfall chart, like the total unit price by month and category in this report. To create this chart, take the following actions:

- Open the Visualizations pane and expand the waterfall chart settings.
- Drag the Month field to the Category entry in the waterfall chart settings from the Fields pane to the right of the Visualizations window.
- A date hierarchy with Year, Quarter, Month, and Day possibilities is displayed when a Month field is added to the Category entry.
- From the date hierarchy, choose the month.
- Drag the Category field to the Breakdown item to add a categorized breakdown to the image.
- Move the Y Axis entry to the Total Units This Year box.

  The Total Units This Year metric you previously generated is referred to in this example as Total Units This Year. To recap, the syntax for this measure is as follows:

  CALCULATE([TotalUnits], Sales[ScenarioID]=1 = Total Units This Year

You'll notice that a tooltip displays as you move your mouse pointer over the different graphic components.

HOW TO CREATE A BUBBLE CHART

The volume of data for different categories—in this case, the variance in overall sales, the average price per unit this year, and the sales per category for the current year—is depicted by a bubble chart. Use these procedures to generate this chart:

- Open the Visualizations pane and expand the bubble chart options.
- Drag the Category field to the Details item in the bubble chart settings after selecting it in the Fields pane to the right of the Visualizations pane.
- To access the Legend entry, drag the Category field.
- To the X Axis entry, drag the Total Sales Variance field.
- Move the Avg $/Unit TY field to the item on the Y Axis.
- To access the Size entry, drag the This Year Sales field.

Once more, a tooltip appears when you move your mouse pointer over the different graphic components.

HOW TO CREATE A LINE CHART

A line chart is the most effective approach to display current year sales by district manager and category. Take these actions:

- Open the Visualizations pane and expand the line chart settings.
- Drag the DM field to the Axis entry in the line chart settings after selecting it in the Fields pane to the right of the Visualizations pane.
- To access the Legend entry, drag the Category field.
- Drag the Values entry to the This Year's Sales field. The final image, complete with tooltip support, is displayed.

HOW TO PUT THE VISUALS IN ORDER

You can rearrange and resize the visualizations in your report as needed once you've added all the ones you need.

- A visual can be moved by clicking anywhere within it and dragging it to the appropriate spot.
- Click inside a visual to change its size.
- Then, to make the image smaller or larger, click either of the corner handles or frame handles, which are located on the image's edge, and drag inward or outward, accordingly.

HOW TO GET THE REPORT READY FOR MOBILE VIEWING

You should prepare your report appropriately if you wish to make it accessible via the Power BI app on an iOS, Android, or Windows mobile device. The steps are as follows to review:

- Select the Phone Layout button under the View tab in Desktop view of the Report window. A mobile device-shaped blank canvas appears.
- Drag a visual from the Visualizations pane to the empty canvas by clicking on it.
- Continue step 2 until the mobile canvas displays every desired image.
- Adjust the images' size and placement as needed.
- Click the View tab and select Desktop Layout to return to Desktop view.

HOW TO VIEW AND PUBLISH THE REPORT

The last stage is to make your report available to the general audience. Here are the actions you must perform in order to review:

- Select Publish from the File menu, then Publish to Power BI.
- The page to publish to Power BI appears.

- Choose the workplace where the report will be published.
- Next, press the "Select" button.
- A dialog box for progress appears. After the procedure is finished, a success message will appear.
- You can confirm that the report shows in the chosen workspace by logging into your Power BI service account after publishing it.
- The Power BI app on your iOS, Android, or Windows mobile device can also be used to view the report.

HOW TO CREATE A DASHBOARD USING THE DATA

Visuals from Power BI reports can be combined to create a unique dynamic dashboard. To evaluate, use these actions to add a visual to a dashboard in a report:

- To add a graphic to a dashboard, open the report that has it.
- Click the Pin Visual icon that shows up in the top-right corner of the image you wish to add to the dashboard after moving your mouse pointer over it. The dialog box for "Pinning to Dashboard" opens.

- Choose the New Dashboard option button and enter a name for the new dashboard to build a new one for the visual.
- As an alternative, pick the preferred dashboard by clicking the Existing Dashboard choice button.
- To add the image to the dashboard, click the Pin button.

HOW TO CREATE REPORTS USING POWER BI FROM SHAREPOINT ONLINE

Creating Power BI reports that use SharePoint Online as their data source is covered in this chapter. SharePoint is typically used for collaboration and document management

You will generate two reports: one from **a SharePoint Online folder** and one from a **SharePoint Online list**.

- **A SharePoint Online list**: As the name implies, is used to store data in list format.
- **A SharePoint Online folder**: On the other hand, keeps data in a document library.

HOW TO USE POWER BI TO IMPORT DATA FROM A SHAREPOINT ONLINE LIST

You begin by loading the lists from SharePoint Online into Power BI. The relationship between the lists must then be established in order to guarantee that the data in the lists will flow seamlessly into the Power BI report. Take these actions:

- In Power BI Desktop, select the Home tab.
- Select "Get Data."
- Select SharePoint Online List under Online Services.
- Type in the URL of the SharePoint Online site where the lists you wish to use to create a Power BI report are located.
- Click the Microsoft Account authentication link to log in to the SharePoint Online website.

OR

- Select Sign In, and provide your login credentials.
- Press the Connect button.
- Decide which lists you wish to import (Expense Budgets and Cost) and select Load.
- All of the lists' internal and external columns are loaded by Power BI. If there is a column in either file that you would prefer not to have in your report, right-click on it and select Delete

There is a single column shared by both lists: Budget Key. You can manually create this relationship if Power BI is unable to identify it automatically. This procedure is reviewed in the steps that follow.

- Select Manage Relationships from Power BI Desktop's Home tab.
- Click the New button on the Manage Relationships page.
- Choose the first list you wish to add to the connection by opening the top drop-down list on the Create connection screen.
- Next, decide which column you wish to use as the foundation for the relationship. To access the bottom drop-down list, repeat step above.
- Press OK.

A relationship is established between the two lists by Power BI.

HOW TO INCLUDE POWER BI GRAPHICS IN THE REPORT

You may improve your Power BI report with visuals. You will include the following images in this area of your report:

- **Slicer:** To filter by budget period and spending category, you will utilize a slicer.

- **A waterfall chart:** The entire costs by date will be displayed in a waterfall chart.
- **The area chart**: The overall spending by budget period and expense category will be displayed in an area chart.
- **A ribbon chart**: A ribbon chart will be used to display the budget by time and spending category.
- **Funnel chart**: You will use a funnel chart to display the budget by category of expenses.
- **The matrix:** The budget period, expense categories, total expenses, budget, and budget used will all be included in a matrix.

HOW TO FILTER WITH SLICER (CATEGORY OF EXPENSES AND BUDGET PERIOD)

You can filter data according to various categories by using a slicer. Here, a slicer that filters data by budget period and spending category will be added. Take these actions to produce this image:

- Open the Visualizations pane and expand the slicer settings.
- Drag the Budget Period field to the Field entry in the slicer settings after selecting it in the Fields pane.

- In the slicer settings, drag the Expense Category field from the Fields pane to the Field entry.
- In the Visualizations window, click the paint roller symbol. Then, choose Horizontal from the Orientation drop-down list.

HOW TO USE WATERFALL CHART

The waterfall chart shows the entire costs by date. You can display time-based data with ongoing computations using a waterfall chart, like the total expenses by date in this report. To create this chart, take the following actions:

- Open the Visualizations pane and expand the waterfall chart settings.
- In the waterfall chart settings, choose the Date field in the Fields pane and drag it to the Category entry.
- Move the field for total expenses to the Y Axis entry.

HOW TO USE AREA CHART (TOTAL SPENDING BY CATEGORY AND BUDGET PERIOD)

Volumes and other value changes over time are displayed in an area chart. The procedures below can be used to construct an area chart that displays changes in total spending by budget period and expense category:

- Open the Visualizations pane and expand the area chart settings.
- In the area chart settings, choose the Budget Period field in the Fields pane and drag it to the Axis entry.
- Move the Legend field beneath the Expense Category field.
- Move the Values field beneath the Total Expenses field.

HOW TO USE RIBBON CHART (BUDGET BY PERIOD AND SPENDING CATEGORY)

A ribbon chart can be used to display the budget by time and spending category. Take these actions:

- Open the Visualizations pane and expand the ribbon chart settings.
- Drag the Expense Category field to the Axis after selecting it in the Fields window.
- Move the Legend field beneath the Budget Period field.
- Drag the Value field beneath the Budget Used field.

HOW TO USE FUNNEL CHART (BUDGET BY CATEGORY OF EXPENSES)

To display the budget by type of expenses, include a funnel chart in the report. Take these actions:

- Open the Visualizations pane and expand the funnel chart settings.
- Drag the Expense Category field to the Group after selecting it in the Fields window.
- Move the Values field beneath the Budget field.

HOW TO USE MATRIX (BUDGET, BUDGET USED, BUDGET PERIOD, SPENDING CATEGORIES, AND TOTAL EXPENSES)

Include a matrix in the report to communicate details such the budget period, spending categories, total expenses, budget, and budget utilized. Take these actions:

- Open the Visualizations pane and expand the matrix settings.
- In the matrix settings, select the Budget Period and Expense Category fields in the Fields pane and drag them to the Rows entry.
- Drag the Budget, Budget Used, and Total Expenses fields from the Fields pane to the Values entry in the matrix settings.

PUT THE VISUALS IN ORDER

Once your report has all the required visualizations, you can arrange them however you like. You can also format your report to be viewed on a mobile device.

VIEW AND PUBLISH THE REPORT

The last stage is to make your report available to the general audience. Here are the actions you must perform in order to review:

- Select Publish from the File menu, then Publish to Power BI.
- The page to publish to Power BI appears. Choose the workplace where the report will be published. Next, press the "Select" button.
- A dialog box for progress appears. Once the process is finished, a success message will appear.

You can confirm that the report shows in the chosen workspace by logging into your Power BI service account after publishing it. The Power BI app on your iOS, Android, or Windows mobile device can also be used to view the report.

CHAPTER SEVEN

CREATE A DASHBOARD USING THE REPORT

Visuals from Power BI reports can be combined to create a unique dynamic dashboard. To review, add a visual in a report to a dashboard by following these steps:

- To add a graphic to a dashboard, open the report that has it.
- Click the Pin Visual icon that shows up in the top-right corner of the image you wish to add to the dashboard after moving your mouse pointer over it. The dialog box for "Pinning to Dashboard" opens.
- Choose the New Dashboard option button and give the new dashboard a name to create a new dashboard for the visual. As an alternative, click the Existing Dashboard option button and pick the dashboard of your choice.
- To add the image to the dashboard, click the Pin button.

HOW TO BUILD A POWER BI REPORT BASED ON DATA FROM A SHAREPOINT ONLINE FOLDER

In addition to creating reports based on data from a SharePoint Online list, you may build them from data from a SharePoint Online folder, such as a document library. In this example, data in a document library called Informative Documents is used to build the report.

To start, you must load data from the SharePoint Online folder into Power BI. Take these actions:

- In Power BI Desktop, select the Home tab.
- Select "Get Data."
- Select the SharePoint Folder after choosing Online Services.
- To build a Power BI report, enter the URL of the SharePoint Online site that houses the folder.
- Click the Microsoft Account authentication option, click Sign In, and then input your username and password to access the SharePoint Online site.
- Press the Connect button.
- Every file in the SharePoint folder will be visible to you. Click Load to import them into Power BI.

Only the information found in the Informative Documents document library should be used as the source data for this report. You will use Power BI's Edit Query option to accomplish this. Take these actions:

- Navigate to Power BI Desktop's Data view.

- To open the Edit Query window, select Edit Query. A preview of the loaded, a query settings pane, and a queries pane are all included in this window.
- In the Queries pane, pick the query you wish to modify.
- In the Ribbon's Query section, select the Advanced Editor option.
- You can modify the chosen query in the Edit Query window that appears.

Modify the query's Source line to look like this: SharePoint is the source. Your SharePoint tenant's name is represented by:

Source = SharePoint.Contents("https://{your-tenant-name}.sharepoint.com/sites/demo/ powerbidemo/", [ApiVersion = 15]),

- Select "Done."

It's time to use the Information Documents document library to create a report. Take these actions:

- Click the Informative Documents entry in the Name column in Data view.
- Then, click the Table entry that corresponds to it in the Content column.

- Next to Informative Documents, select the Table entry.
- To apply the modifications to the data model, click the Close and Apply button on the Ribbon.

HOW TO INCLUDE POWER BI VISUALS IN THE REPORT

You can include images in this report, just like you did with the one you made earlier in this chapter. These could consist of the following:

- **Slicer:** To filter by file extension, you'll use a slicer.
- **A multi-row card:** The number of files by extension will be displayed on a multi-row card.
- **Pie chart**: The number of files per extension is also displayed in a pie chart.
- **The date filter slicer**: For date filters, you'll add two slicers: one for sorting files by creation date and another for sorting files by modification date.
- **Table**: A list of files together with their folder path, extension, creation and modification dates will be included in a table.

Use these procedures to add a slicer that filters data based on file extension:

- Open the Visualizations pane and expand the slicer settings.
- Drag the Extension field to the Field entry in the slicer settings after selecting it in the Fields pane.

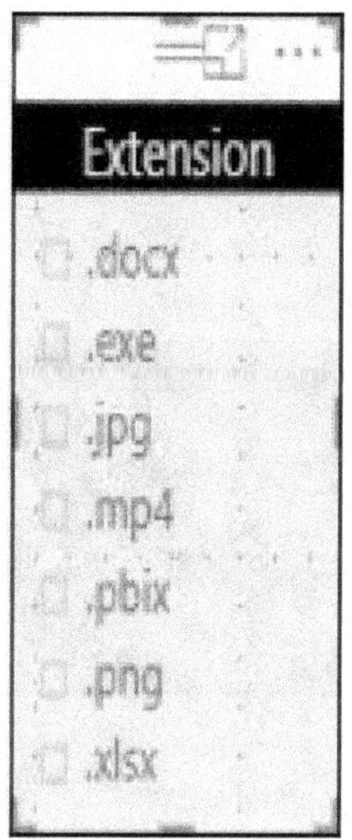

MULTI-ROW CARD (EXTENSION-BASED FILE COUNT):

You will need to add a multi-row card in order to show the file count by extension. Take these actions:

- Open the Visualizations pane and expand the multi-row card options.
- Drag the Extension field to the Fields item in the multi-row card settings after selecting it in the Fields pane.
- Move the field labeled "Count of File Name" beneath the "Extension" field.

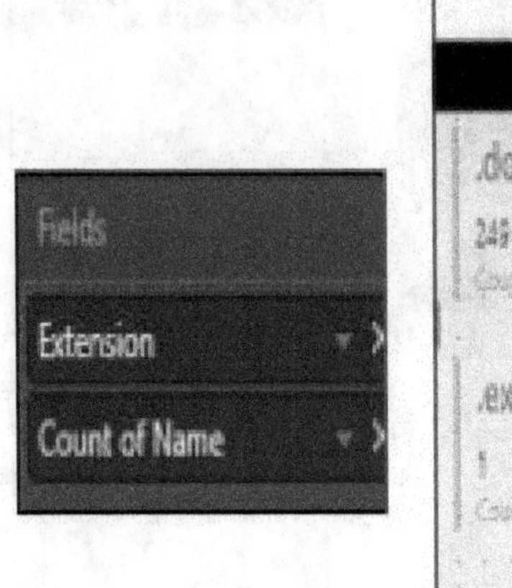

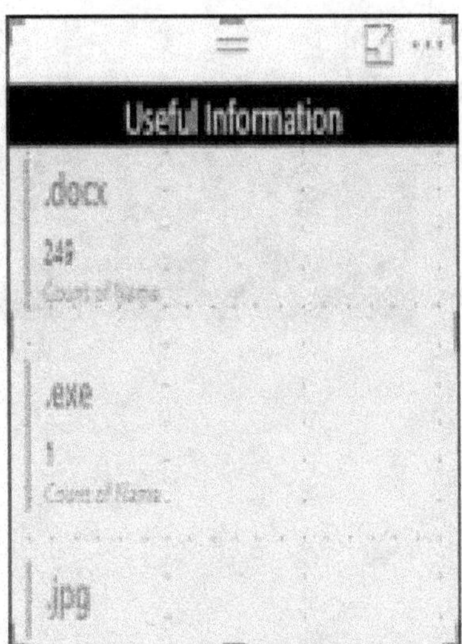

PIE CHART WITH THE NUMBER OF FILES BY EXTENSION:

Use these procedures to display the file count by extension in pie chart form:

- Open the Visualizations pane and expand the pie chart settings.
- In the pie chart settings, select the Extension field in the Fields pane and drag it to the Legend entry.
- In the pie chart settings, choose the Count of Name field in the Fields pane and drag it to the Values entry.

DATE FILTER SLICER (CREATED DATE, MODIFIED DATE)

Here, you'll add two date filter slicers: one for sorting by creation date and another for sorting by modification date. Take these actions:

- In the Visualizations pane, expand the date settings slicer.
- Drag the Date Created field from the Fields pane to the Date Settings slicer's Field entry.
- For the Date Modified field, repeat steps 1 and 2.

TABLE (NAME, LOCATION TO THE FOLDER, EXTENSION, CREATION DATE, MODIFICATION DATE)

Use these procedures to generate a table including file names, folder directories, file extensions, and the dates they were created and modified:

- Open the Visualizations pane and expand the table settings.
- Drag the Date Created, Date Modified, Folder Path, Extension, and Name entries from the entries pane to the Values entry in the table settings.

Put the images in order. Once your report has all the required graphics, you can organize them anyway you choose

VIEW AND PUBLISH THE REPORT

The last stage is to make your report available to the general audience

CREATE A DASHBOARD USING THE DATA

Visuals from Power BI reports can be combined to create a unique dynamic dashboard.

HOW TO REFRESH THE POWER BI REPORT'S DATA

To display the most recent data, you can set up your report to refresh automatically. Here's how:

- Launch the Power BI application.
- Launch the workspace (in this case, Temp Workspace) containing the report you wish to have automatically refreshed.

- Click the ellipsis that appears after moving your mouse pointer over the report you wish to refresh in the Datasets section (in this case, Power BI Report

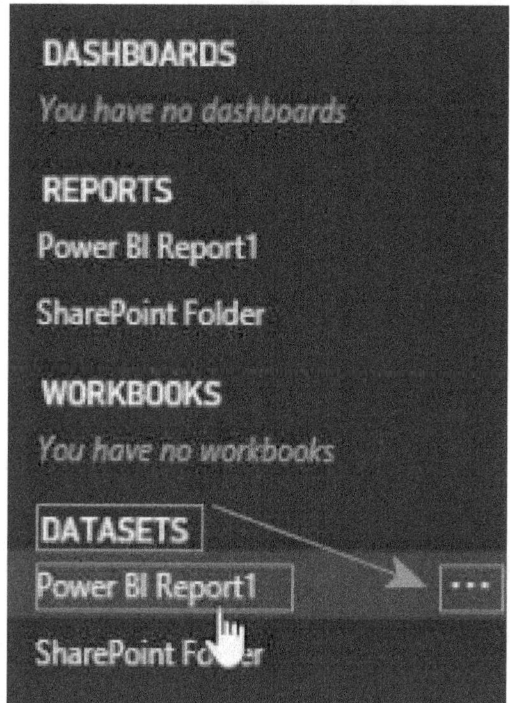

- Press the Schedule Refresh button
- Expand the Gateway Connection section in the resulting window. Since all of the dataset's data sources are in the cloud, Power BI indicates that you don't require a gateway for this dataset. However, if you want more control over your connection, you can utilize a gateway.

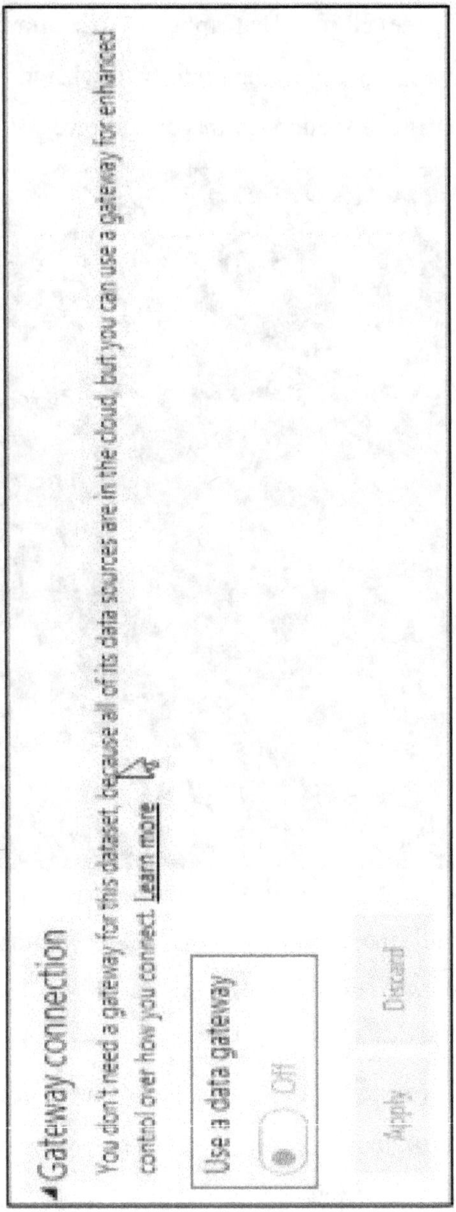

Gateway connection

You don't need a gateway for this dataset, because all of its data sources are in the cloud, but you can use a gateway for enhanced control over how you connect. Learn more

Use a data gateway

Off

Apply Discard

- Click the Edit Credential option after expanding the Data Source section. You can sign in to the SharePoint Online website when a window opens.
- Select OAuth2 from the Authentication Method drop-down list.
- Enter your username and password after clicking the Sign In button.
- Once your login has been successful, you will get a message that says "Data Source Updated" when you return to the Schedule Refresh page.
- Toggle the Keep Your Data Up to Date option to On under Scheduled Refresh.

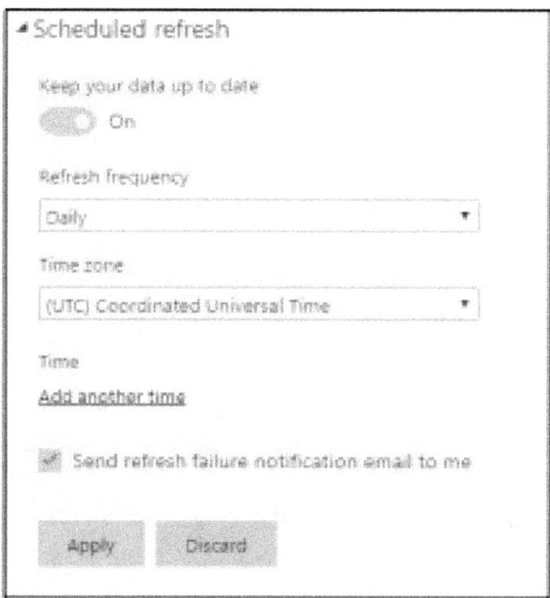

- Choose how frequently you wish to refresh the data by opening the Refresh Frequency drop-down box.
- Select your time zone by opening the Time Zone drop-down list.
- Select "Apply."

Use these steps to determine when the last refresh took place:

- Select the source of data.
- To view comprehensive details about recent schedule refresh procedures, click the Refresh History link.

INTEGRATE REPORTS FROM POWER BI INTO SHAREPOINT ONLINE

If you have a Power BI Pro subscription, you can integrate reports you produce in Power BI into a SharePoint Online page. Here's how:

- Open the Power BI report that you wish to incorporate in the Power BI service.
- Select Embed in SharePoint Online from the File menu.
- A URL is displayed by Power BI. To embed the report in SharePoint Online, use this URL.
- Make a copy of the URL.

- Navigate to the SharePoint Online page where the report is to be embedded.
- From the menu that displays, choose Power BI after clicking the Add button.

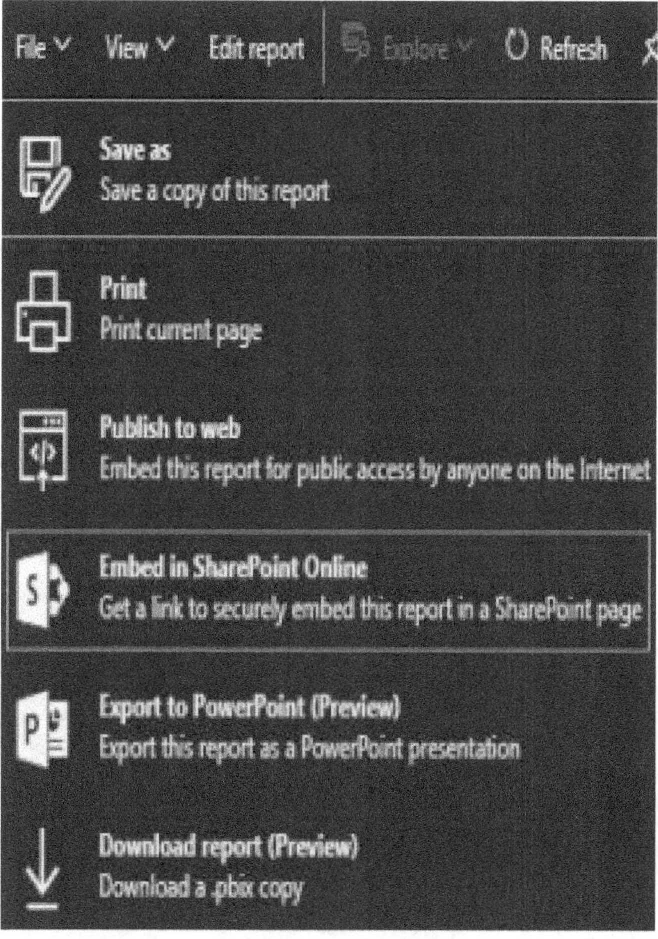

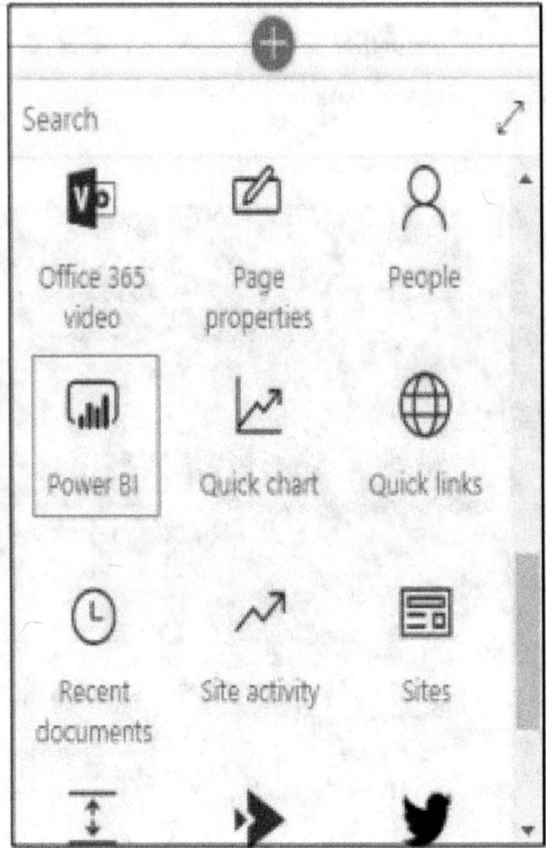

- Press "Add Report."
- A window for Power BI opens.
- Paste the URL you copied in step 3 into the Power BI

- Select which report page the user should view first by opening the Page Name drop-down box.

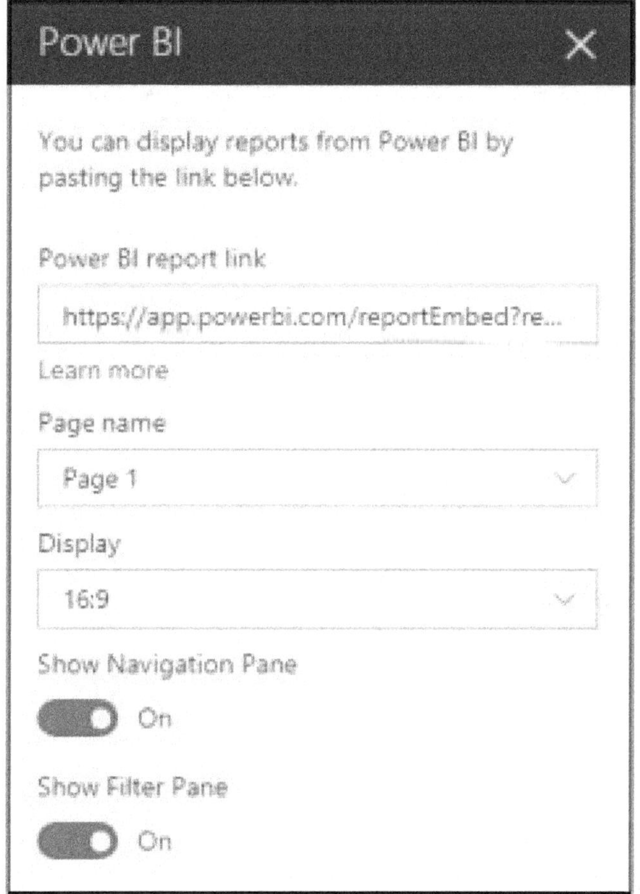

- Select a display setting by opening the Display drop-down menu. The report's placement on the

SharePoint Online page will be determined by this parameter.

- Toggle the Navigation Pane setting to On to display the report's navigation pane. Toggle the option to Off to hide the pane.
- Toggle the Filter Pane setting to On to display the report's filter pane. Toggle the option to Off to hide the pane.

Data refresh capabilities are offered by the Power BI service at predetermined times. This aids in updating Power BI reports and data sources appropriately.

HOW TO CREATE POWER BI REPORTS WITH ON-PREMISES SHAREPOINT

Use these procedures to import data into Power BI from SharePoint On-Premises lists:

- In Power BI Desktop, select the Home tab.
- Select "Get Data."
- Pick SharePoint List under Other.

- Type in the address of the SharePoint On-Premises site where the lists you wish to use to create a Power

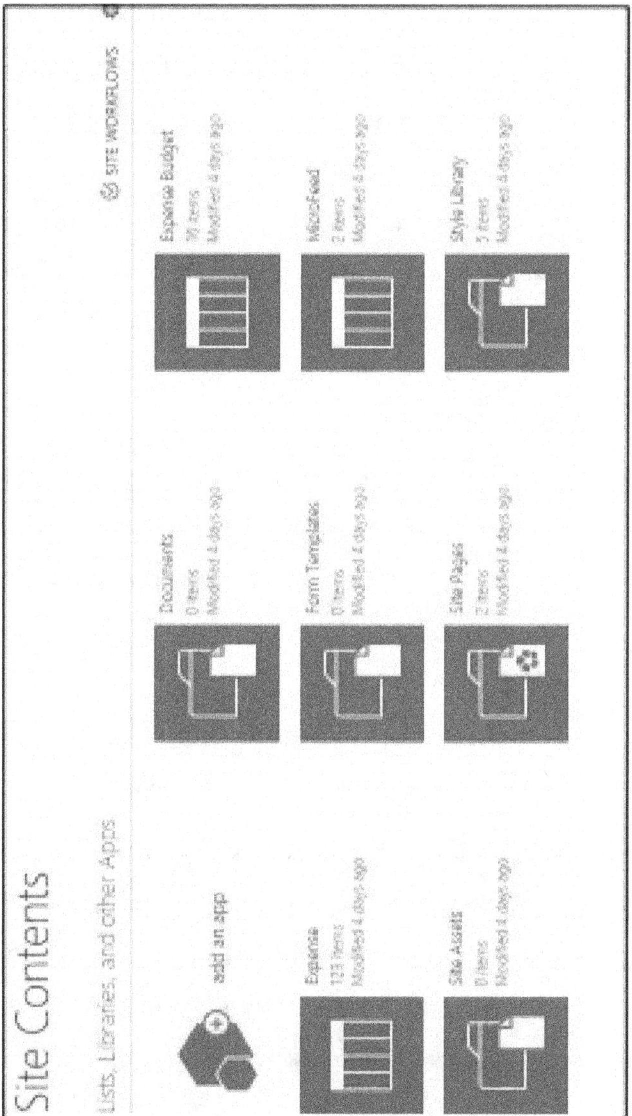

BI report are located.

- If SharePoint On-Premises is installed locally, click the Use My Current Credentials option button after selecting Windows as the login method when requested.
- As an alternative, choose the Use Alternate Credentials option button and type the preferred username and password in the corresponding boxes if SharePoint On-Premises is installed on a different computer.
- Press the Connect button.
- Click Load after selecting the files you wish to import (Expense Budget and Expense in this case).
- All of the files' internal and external columns are loaded by Power BI.
- Right-click on any column in either file and select Delete if you don't want it in your report.

HOW TO MAKE A REPORT USING POWER BI

Similar to creating a report from a SharePoint Online list, you can create a Power BI report from a SharePoint On-Premises list. We will utilize the same report you produced prior instead of repeating those steps here.

INSTALL A DATA GATEWAY

To create a safe connection between Power BI and SharePoint On-Premises, you utilize a data gateway. Power BI reports created from SharePoint On-Premises data stay current thanks to this safe connection. The gateway essentially serves as a link between Power BI and SharePoint On-Premises (as well as other Microsoft products like Microsoft Flow, Logic Apps, and PowerApps). A data gateway needs to be installed on your computer in order to be used.

The following minimal specifications must be fulfilled by this machine:

.NET 4.6 Framework

64-bit Windows 7 or Windows Server 2008 R2 or later (Windows 2012 R2 or later 64-bit versions are advised). Microsoft also suggests that your computer have an 8-core CPU and at least 8 GB of memory.

WHAT TO REMEMBER BEFORE INSTALLING THE DATA GATEWAY

Prior to configuring the data gateway, you need to publish your report to the Power BI service.

- To use the data gateway, you do not require Analysis Services.
- An Analysis Services data source can be accessed using the gateway.
- A data gateway cannot be installed on a domain controller.
- Installing a data gateway on a laptop or PC that might shut off, go to sleep, or be unplugged from the Internet is not a good idea.
- The computer on which the data gateway is installed needs to be a member of the same AD as the data source in order to use Windows Authentication.

HOW TO SET UP THE DATA GATEWAY

To install a data gateway, take the following actions:

- Type http://go(dot)microsoft(dot)com/fwlink/?LinkID=820925 into the browser. Enter the address box of your web browser to start the data gateway installer.
- Click Open after doing a right-click on the installation.
- The installation will then begin when you click Next.
- You are prompted by the installer to choose the kind of data gateway that you wish to install.

Two options are available to you:

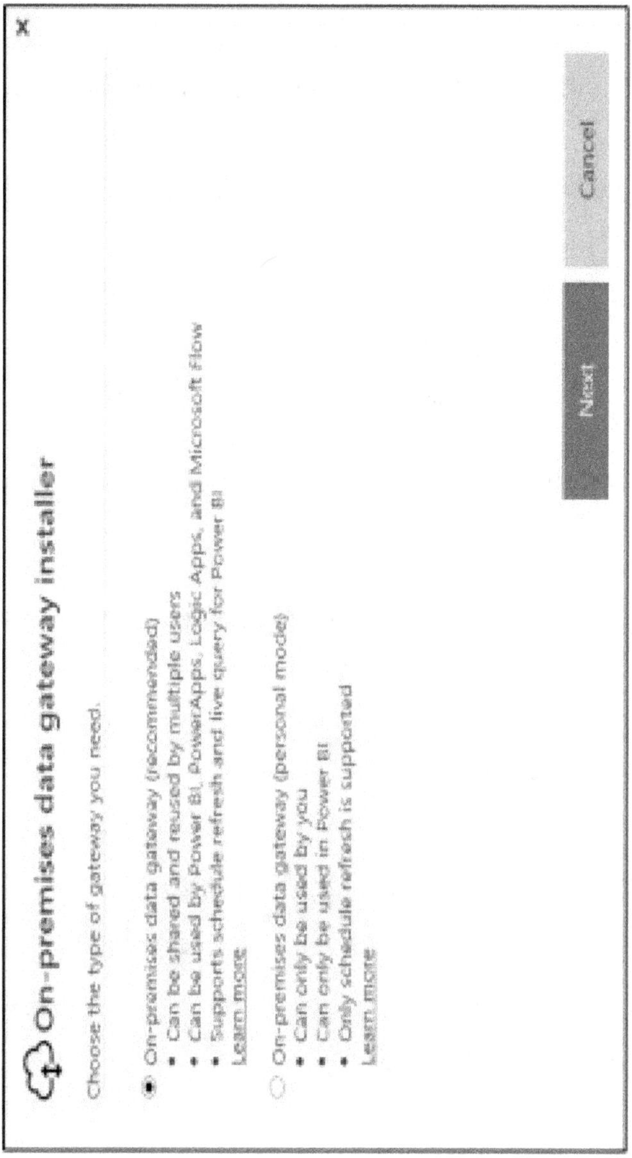

On-premises data gateway installer

Choose the type of gateway you need.

On-premises data gateway (recommended)
- Can be shared and reused by multiple users
- Can be used by Power BI, PowerApps, Logic Apps, and Microsoft Flow
- Supports schedule refresh and live query for Power BI

Learn more

On-premises data gateway (personal mode)
- Can only be used by you
- Can only be used in Power BI
- Only schedule refresh is supported

Learn more

Next Cancel

- The On-Premises Data Gateway is advised. Multiple users can share and reuse this kind of gateway, which is compatible with Power BI, PowerApps, Logic Apps, and Microsoft Flow. It also enables live queries and scheduled refreshes. (In the remainder of this book, I will often call this kind of gateway a shared gateway.)
- Personal Mode On-Premises Data Gateway: Only a single user may use this kind of gateway, and it is only compatible with Power BI and scheduled refreshes.

In this instance, click Next after selecting the On-Premises Data Gateway (Recommended) option button. A pop-up window alerts you that the gateway will operate more slowly on a wireless network and advises you to install it on a computer that is constantly on.

- To end the pop-up window, click Next.
- Accept the terms and conditions and proceed with the installation.
- Click Next after that.

- Click Sign In after entering the email address linked to your Power BI Pro account. You are prompted to register the gateway by the installation.
- Give the data gateway a name. You are free to choose any name for this. Enter SharePoint On Premise Gateway in the Name field in this example.
- In the Recovery Key box, type a recovery key. Next, type it again in the box labeled "Confirm Recovery Key."

  A minimum of eight characters must be included in the recovery key. In the event that the data gateway fails, you will use it to recover it.
- Select Configure.
- A notification that the data gateway is online and operational is shown by the installer.

HOW TO EXAMINE THE DATA GATEWAY

Let's take a time to examine the data gateway before configuring Power BI to connect to it. Take these actions to open the data gateway:

- On the Windows desktop, click the Start button.
- In the search box on the Start menu, type gateway.
- Select the data gateway entry from the list that displays.

The following displays are part of the data gateway interface:

- **Status**: This screen shows the data gateway's current state, including whether it is compatible with

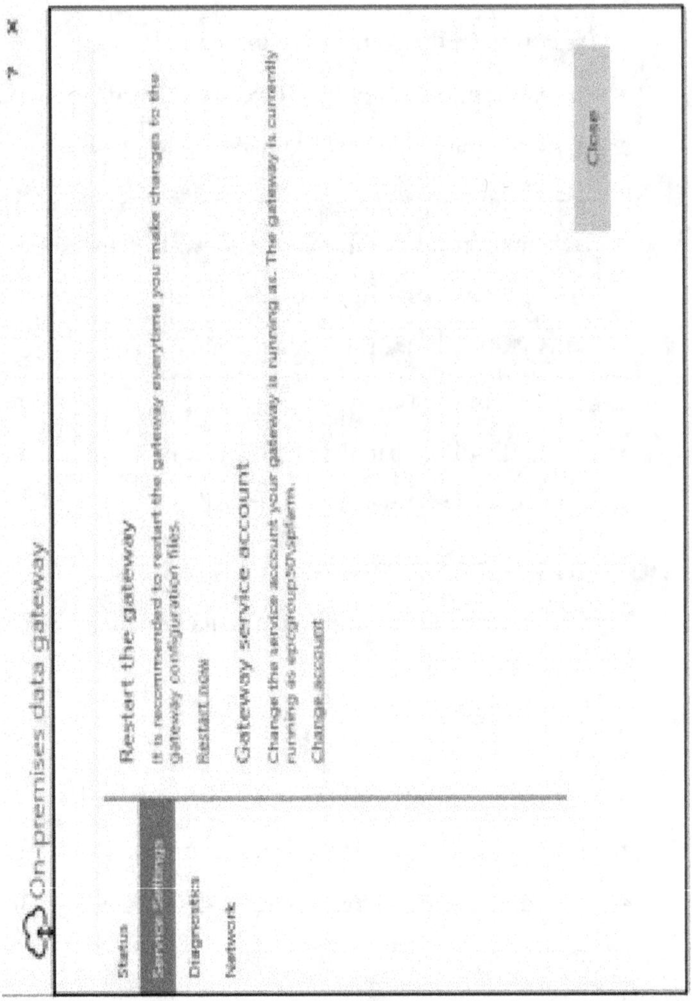

Microsoft Flow, PowerApps, Logic Apps, and Power BI.

- **Service Settings**: This screen has two: Restart and Gateway service account. You have to restart the gateway in order to apply modifications made to the configuration files. Click the **Restart Now** link under Restart the Gateway to accomplish this. Account for Gateway Service: Click the Change Account link under Gateway Service Account to modify the service account linked to the data gateway.

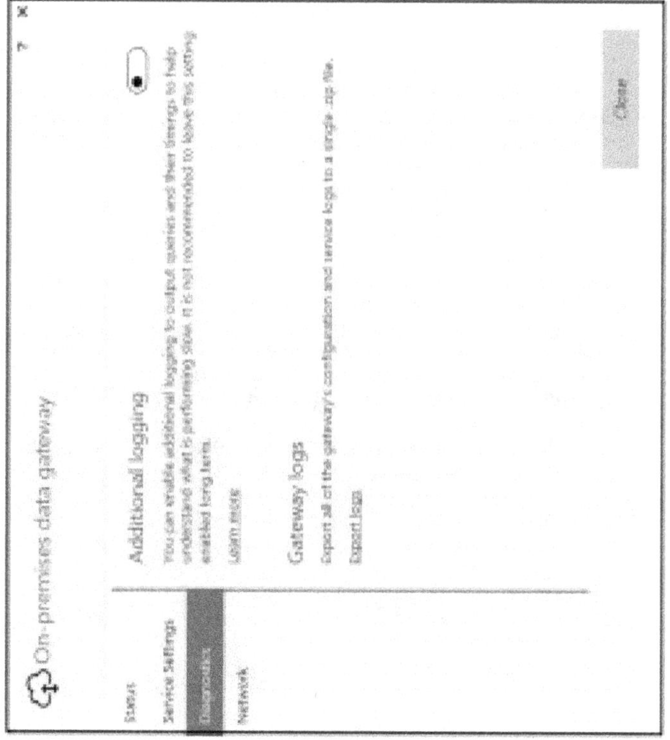

- **Diagnostics**: There are two choices on this screen: **Additional logging**: Turn this option on to evaluate the data gateway's performance more accurately. Click the Learn More option under Additional Logging to find out more about this configuration. **Gateway Logs**: To export all of the data gateway's configuration and service logs to a single ZIP file, click the Export Logs link under Gateway Logs.
- **Network**: This screen has two options related to the data gateway network connection:

  Network Status: This indicates how the network connection is doing. Click the Check Now link under Network Status to see if the gateway is reachable from outside the network.

  HTTPS Mode: Turn this option on to have the gateway use HTTPS rather than TCP for communication. Click the Learn More tab under HTTPS Mode to find out more about these options.

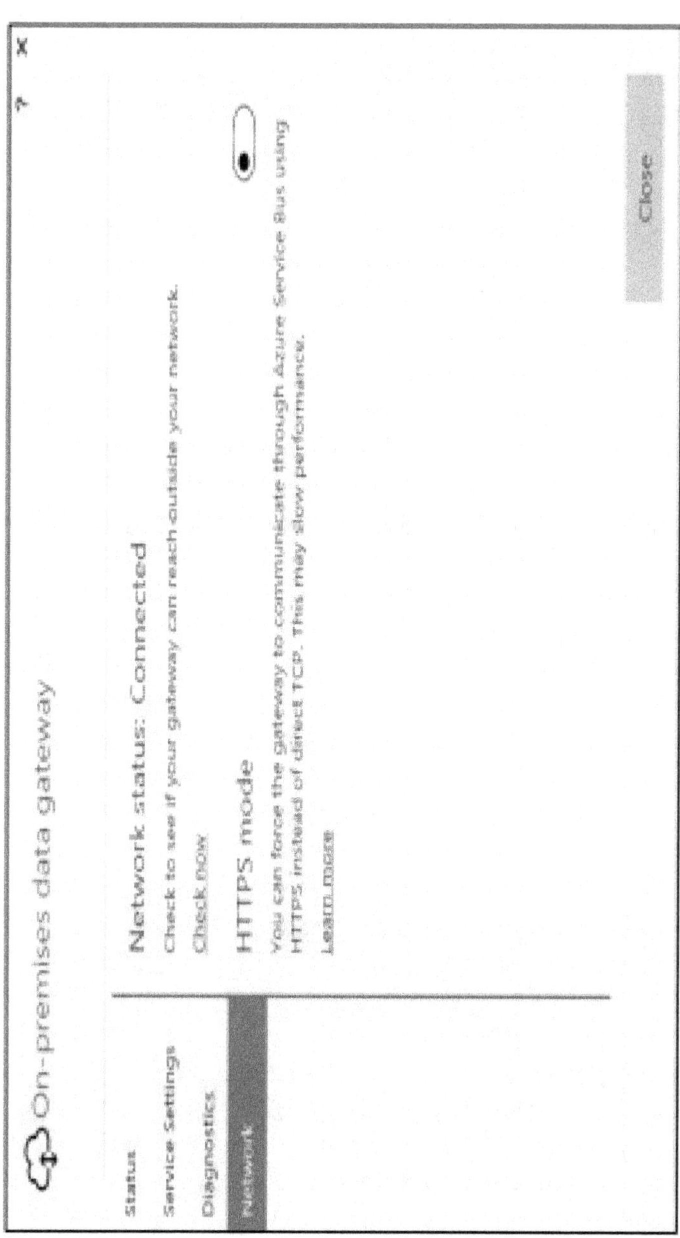
On-premises data gateway
Status
Service Settings
Diagnostics
Network
Network status: Connected
Check to see if your gateway can reach outside your network.
Check now
HTTPS mode
You can force the gateway to communicate through Azure Service Bus using HTTPS instead of direct TCP. This may slow performance.
Learn more
Close

CONFIGURE REFRESH FEATURE AND THE DATA GATEWAY IN POWER BI

Refresh history

◢Gateway connection

To use a data gateway, make sure the computer is online and the data source is added in Manage Gateways.

A new personal gateway is available to connect to on-premises data. Install now Learn more

◉ Use your data gateway (personal mode)

○ Use a data gateway

Apply Discard

You must setup Power BI to use your data gateway after it has been set up. Take these actions:

- Sign in to the Power BI platform.
- Hover your mouse pointer over the expense report you made using SharePoint On-Premises data under Datasets. Click the ellipsis that shows, then select Schedule Refresh.
- Click the Manage Gateways option after expanding the Gateway Connection section in the report's Settings box.
- The window for Gateway Cluster Settings opens.
- Select "Add Data Sources to Use the Gateway" from the menu.
- In the Data Source Name box, enter the name of the data source.
- Select SharePoint from the Data Source Type drop-down menu.
- In the SharePoint Site URL box, type the SharePoint site's URL.
- Select Windows from the Authentication Method drop-down selection.
- In the Username box, enter your SharePoint On-Premises username.

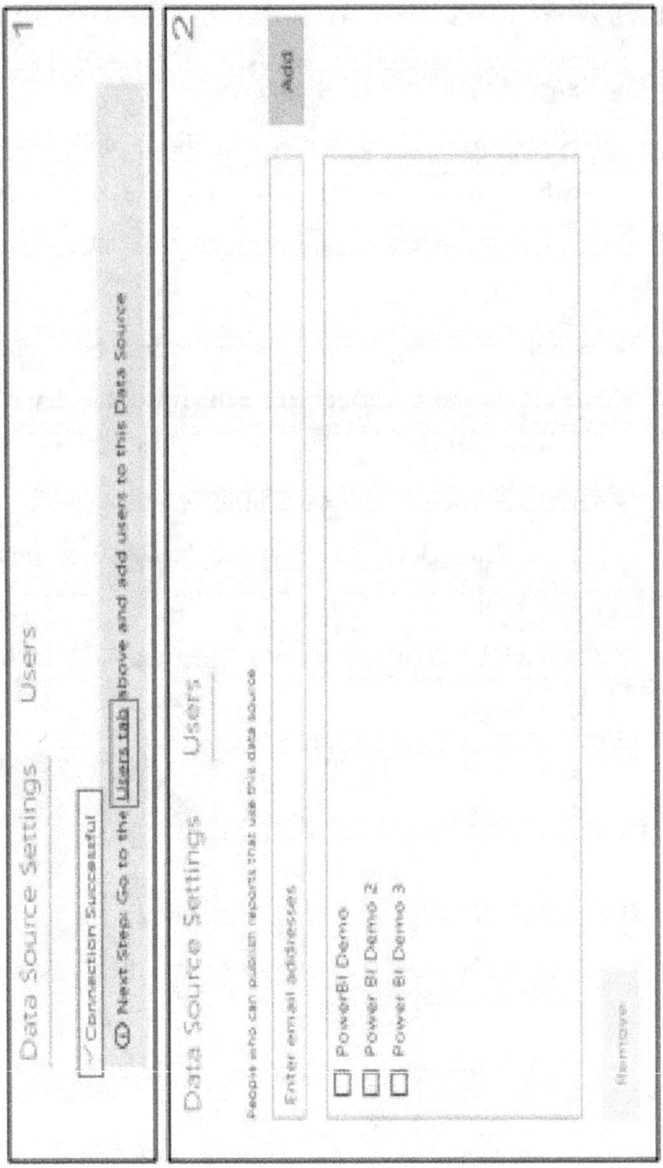

1

Data Source Settings Users

✓ Connection Successful

ⓘ Next Step: Go to the Users tab above and add users to this Data Source

2

Data Source Settings Users

People who can publish reports that use this data source

Enter email addresses

Add

☐ PowerBI Demo

☐ Power BI Demo 2

☐ Power BI Demo 3

Remove

In the Password box, enter your password.

- Select "Add."
- The successful connection to the data gateway should be shown in the Data Source Settings pane. The next thing you need to do is define who can use the data gateway.
- Select the tab for Users In the People Who Can Publish Reports That Use This Data Source box, enter the email address of the person you want to grant access to the data gateway, then click Add.
- Choose the gateway you wish to use, click Apply, and then click the Use a Data Gateway option button under Gateway Connection in the report's Settings box.
- After selecting "Use a Data Gateway," click "Apply."
- An Updated Connection notification will appear.
- To view the connection's status, expand the Data Source Credentials section in the Settings pane.

◢ Data source credentials

SharePoint (admin has granted access, credentials are not required)

- The last step is to configure the data gateway to automatically refresh the report.
- Open the Settings window and expand the Scheduled Refresh section.
- Select "Keep Your Data Up to Date" from the menu.
- Choose how frequently you wish to refresh the data by using the Refresh Frequency drop-down box.
- Select your time zone by using the Time Zone drop-down list.
- Select "Apply."

CHAPTER EIGHT

CREATE POWER BI REPORTS WITH SQL

The creation of a Power BI report that uses information from a SQL Server database as its source will be covered in this chapter. In addition, you will learn how to set up and configure a data gateway that will allow Power BI users to access SQL Server database data via a live database connection and schedule refresh operations. Additionally, you will learn how to set up Row-Level Security (RLS) so that only authorized users can access the report.

HOW TO USE POWER BI TO IMPORT DATA FROM A SQL SERVER DATABASE

Data from a SQL Server database can be imported into Power BI in two different ways:

- **Import mode:** Data is cached from the database into Power BI when you import it using import mode. You must regularly refresh the data to make sure you are working with the most recent version.
- **DirectQuery mode**: Data is not directly imported into Power BI by DirectQuery. Instead, it keeps the SQL Server database and Power BI connected. This data will be updated in real time when you use it to create a report in Power BI.

HOW TO USE IMPORT MODE TO IMPORT DATA

Use import mode to import data into Power BI from a SQL Server database by doing the following:

- In Power BI Desktop, select the Home tab.
- Select "Get Data."
- Select the SQL Server database under Database.
- Press the Connect button. The window for the SQL Server Database opens.
- In the Server Name box, enter the name of the SQL Server that you wish to import data from.
- In the Database Name box, enter the name of the database from which you wish to import data.
- Choose Import from the Data Connectivity Mode menu.
- Press OK.
- Select Database when asked to choose the authentication mechanism.
- Enter the SQL Server database's username in the Username box.
- Enter the relevant password in the Password box.
- Press the Connect button. A preview of the chosen table will appear on the right, while a list of every

table that is available in the Azure SQL database will appear on the left.

- Click Load after selecting the tables you wish to import. The tables are imported into Power BI Desktop, which uses them to create a data model.

HOW TO USE DIRECTQUERY MODE CONNECT TO THE DATA

Here's how to use Power BI's DirectQuery mode to connect to data in a SQL Server database:

- Repeat the previous section's steps 1 through 6.
- Choose the DirectQuery option under Data Connectivity Mode.
- Press OK.
- Select Database when asked to choose the authentication mechanism.
- Enter the SQL Server database's username in the Username box.
- Enter the relevant password in the Password box.
- Select Connect. A list of every table in the SQL Server database will be displayed to you, along with a preview of each one.
- Click Load after selecting the tables you wish to connect to. In contrast to import mode, Power BI

Desktop does not create a data model from the tables it connects to. The reason for this is because Power BI Desktop has a direct connection to the data source.

HOW TO UTILIZE AN INLINE QUERY TO IMPORT DATA

An inline SQL query can also be used to import data into Power BI from a SQL Server database. Both import mode and DirectQuery mode imports can be performed using inline SQL queries. You can do an import mode action using an inline query by following these steps:

- Repeat steps 1 through 7 from the "Import data using import mode" section.
- In the SQL Server Database window, expand the Advanced Options area and enter the following inline query:

```
Select sp.[SalesQuota]
    ,sp.[Bonus]
    ,sp.[CommissionPct]
    ,sp.[SalesYTD]
    ,sp.[SalesLastYear]
    ,st.[Name]
```

FROM [Sales].[SalesPerson] as sp inner join[Sales].[SalesTerritory] as st

on

sp.[TerritoryID]=st.[TerritoryID].

- You can choose to use the Navigate Using Full Hierarchy and Include Relationship Columns checkboxes.
- Press OK.
- Select Database when asked to choose the authentication mechanism.
- Enter the Oracle database username in the User Name field.
- Enter the relevant password in the Password box.
- Select Connect.
- Click Load after previewing the data columns you specified for import.

Let's begin with the images. Your report should include the following items:

- **Slicer**: To filter data according to department, job title, and shift, you will utilize a slicer.
- **Pie chart**: The number of employees by gender will be displayed in a pie chart.

- **A chart with colored columns:** The number of employees by marital status and gender will be displayed in a clustered column chart.
- **A multi-row card**: A multi-row card will be used to display details about each shift.
- **A bar chart that is stacked**: A stacked bar chart will be used to display the number of employees by gender and job title. Informational data such as the employee's first and last names, phone number, number of sick leave hours, and number of vacation hours will be included in a table.
- **Gauge chart:** The entire number of workers in the company will be displayed on a gauge. Once the images have been added, you can organize them however you like.

HOW TO INSTALL A DATA GATEWAY

To create a safe connection between Power BI and the SQL Server database, you utilize a data gateway. You may maintain the most recent versions of your Power BI reports by using this secure connection. The gateway essentially serves as a link between Power BI and the SQL Server database (as well as other Microsoft products like Microsoft Flow, Logic Apps, and PowerApps). Power BI uses this bridge to update reports using information from the SQL Server database.

Installing and setting up a data gateway for SharePoint On-Premises was covered prior. The system requirements for a data gateway were described, along with the shared and personal data gateway kinds that are available. Additionally, it guided you through the process of configuring a shared data gateway. This section concentrates on installing and configuring a personal data gateway rather than restating all of that information.

HOW TO SET UP A GATEWAY FOR PERSONAL DATA

Take these actions to set up a personal data gateway:

- To start the data gateway installer, type http://go(dot)microsoft(dot)com/fwlink/?LinkID=820925 into the address bar of your web browser.
- Click Open after doing a right-click on the installation. The installation will then begin when you click Next.
- Click Next after selecting the On-Premises Data Gateway (Personal Mode) option button.
- A pop-up window alerts you that the gateway will operate more slowly on a wireless network and

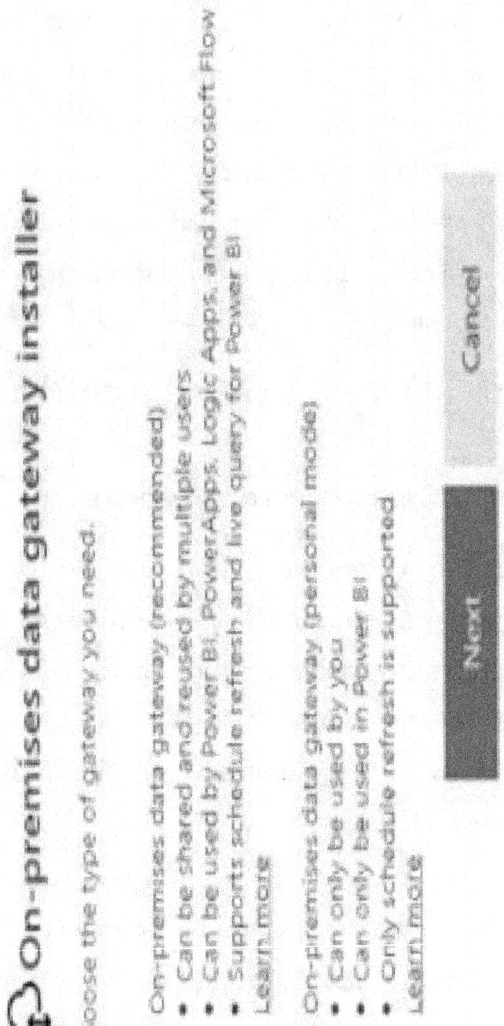

On-premises data gateway installer

Choose the type of gateway you need.

On-premises data gateway (recommended)
- Can be shared and reused by multiple users
- Can be used by Power BI, PowerApps, Logic Apps, and Microsoft Flow
- Supports schedule refresh and live query for Power BI

Learn more

On-premises data gateway (personal mode)
- Can only be used by you
- Can only be used in Power BI
- Only schedule refresh is supported

Learn more

Next Cancel

advises you to install it on a computer that is

constantly on.

- To end the window, click Next

- Accept the terms and conditions and proceed with the installation. Click Next after that.

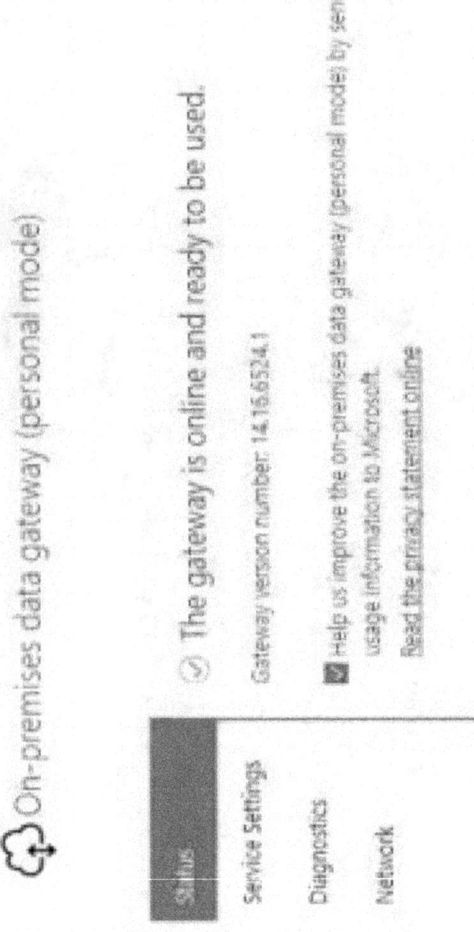

- Click Sign In after entering the email address linked to your Power BI Pro account.
- A notification that the data gateway is online and operational is shown by the installer.

You must setup Power BI to use your own data gateway to refresh your report once you have set it up. The instructions that follow show you how to set up Power BI to use a personal data gateway.

- Sign in to the Power BI platform.
- Move the mouse pointer over the report you made using information from the SQL Server database under Datasets.
- Then, click the ellipsis that shows up and select Schedule Refresh.
- Click the Use Your Data Gateway (Personal Mode) option button, then click Apply after expanding the Gateway Connection section in the report Settings box that appears. The data gateway is connected to Power BI.

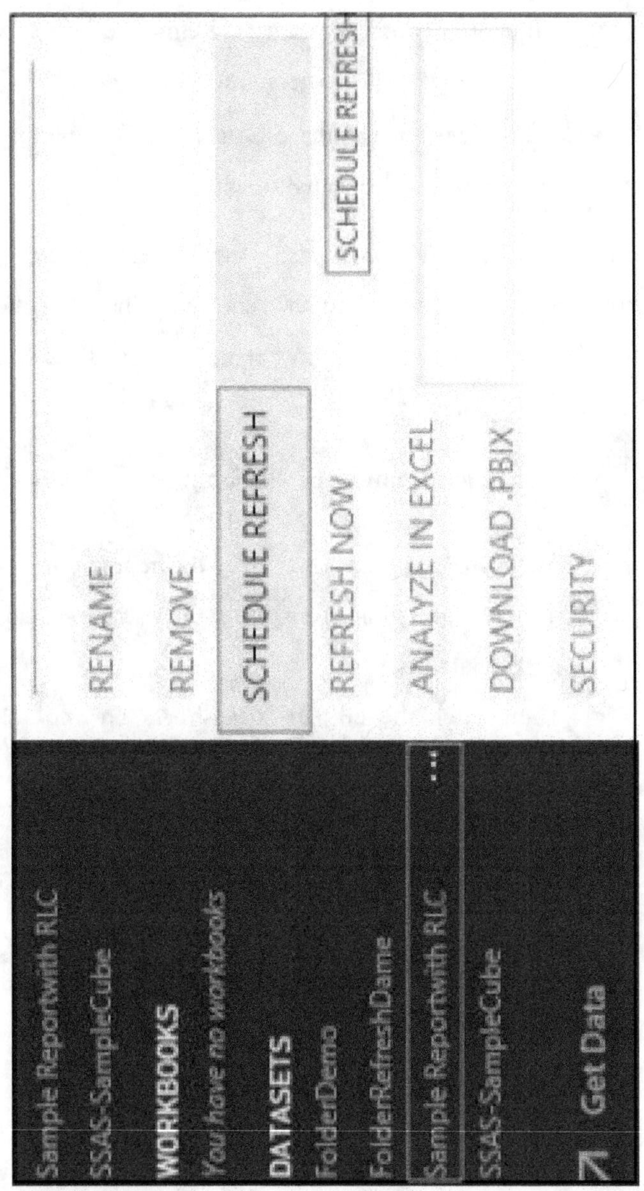

- Next, use the data gateway to set up an automatic

refresh schedule for the report.

- Open the Settings window and expand the Scheduled Refresh section.
- Select "Keep Your Data Up to Date" from the menu.
- Choose how frequently you wish to refresh the data by using the Refresh Frequency drop-down box.
- Select your time zone from the Time Zone drop-down list.
- Select "Apply."

HOW TO SET UP POWER BI'S ROW-LEVEL SECURITY (RLS)

Let's set up Row Level Security (RLS) in a Power BI report now that you've had some experience with the tool. With RLS, you can add user-specific roles to limit who can and cannot access certain data in Power BI.

By default, all users will have access to the tables and fields that support a report that you publish in Power BI. This can be avoided with RLS. Think back to the employee data you used earlier in this chapter to create a report. Let's say you wanted users to be able to view only data from their department. For instance, you desired Viewing staff data from the engineering department is possible, but not from the facilities and maintenance department. You can accomplish this by limiting access to information about members of one department by implementing user-specific roles.

Create and verify the roles you wish to apply to the table as your first step after accessing the report. Take these actions:

- In Power BI Desktop, select the Modeling tab. After that, select Manage Roles under the Security group.
- A dialogue window appears. In the Manage Roles section, click the Create button.
- In the box that appears, type the role's name; in this example, it's Engineering. After that, click Create or hit Enter. The role is created by Power BI, which also displays every table that it can apply to.
- Type the following DAX expression into the table you wish to apply the role to.
- The new position is created by Power BI. 5. To create an Executive job, repeat steps 1-4.
- To develop a marketing role and a finance role, repeat these two more times.
- Select the Modeling tab to verify the role. Next, select the View as Roles button under the Security group.

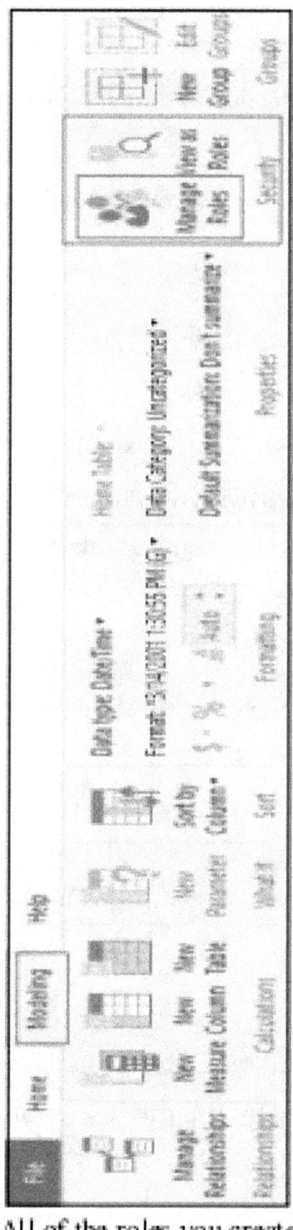

- All of the roles you created are listed in the View as

Roles dialog box. Check the ROLE box. Only department personnel for the role can see employee data thanks to Power BI's filtering of the table contents.

- To go back to the prior view, click Stop Viewing.

Use these procedures to apply a rule to a particular user:

- Select the relevant report under Datasets, and in the resulting box, select Security.
- Assign a user a role. The window for Row-Level Security opens. The roles you defined are listed on the left side of the window, along with the number of individuals assigned to each role, enclosed in parenthesis.
- Click the Engineer entry in the list on the left to give a user the Engineer role.
- Enter the email address of a user you wish to apply for the Engineering job to in the People or Groups Who Belong to This job box on the window's right side.
- Click Add after that.
- The count in parenthesis next to the Engineering entry on the left rises by 1, and the user's name shows

beneath the area where you entered their email address.

- Select "Save."
- Use the login credentials of the person you applied the role to (Joseph) to access the Power BI service. Only the engineering department's employees' data will be visible to you.

RLS'S LIMITATIONS WITH POWER BI

RLS is a powerful tool for protecting your data in Power BI. Nevertheless, it has certain drawbacks:

- In Power BI Desktop, roles and rules need to be defined. This is not possible with Power BI services. However, in Power BI service, you can assign roles to users.
- The dataset you need to restrict must be loaded into Power BI Desktop before you can utilize RLS. For instance, you must import the Excel file into Power BI Desktop in order to apply RLS to a report that uses data from an Excel file.
- RLS has strong support on DirectQuery and ETL platforms. You can use the on-premises model if you are capable of managing real-time connections for analytic services. RLS can be implemented in the on-

premises model, for instance, if you load an SSAS tabular model into Power BI with a live connection.

- RLS is not compatible with Cortana or Q&A.

HOW TO CREATE POWER BI REPORTS USING THE SSAS CUBE

Building a Power BI report using information from a SQL Server Analysis Services (SSAS) cube is here. In order to use the SSAS cube, you will also learn how to configure a data gateway.

BASIC WORDS

Let's go over some fundamental vocabulary first, specifically defining the words "SSAS cube," "measure," and "dimension," before delving into the specifics of creating a report using data from an SSAS cube.

- **Measures** and **dimensions** for data selection make up a SQL Server Analysis Services (SSAS) cube.
- Tables and views in a data source, such a SQL Server database, are the source of these measurements and dimensions.
- Data that is returned from a column's numeric expression is called a **measure**. A measure would be, for instance, the sum of an expression that shows the total sales during a given time period. A measure

group can be created by combining several measures that are taken from different columns in a database.

- The characteristics of the relationship between the measures in a cube are referred to as **dimensions**. These characteristics are taken from columns that are accessible in one or more data-containing tables.
- "A collection of all related objects called attributes which can be used to provide information about fact data in one or more cubes" is how Microsoft defines a dimension.

HOW TO USE POWER BI TO IMPORT DATA FROM AN SSAS CUBE

Use Power BI to import data from an SSAS cube. Data from an SSAS database can be imported into Power BI in two different ways:

- **Import mode:** When you use import mode to import data from an SSAS cube, the data is cached from the database into Power BI, same like when you import data from a SQL Server database. You must regularly refresh the data to make sure you are working with the most recent version.
- **Connect in live mode**: This is quite similar to the DirectQuery mode. You don't explicitly import data

into Power BI while using Connect Live mode. Instead, you continue to connect Power BI to the SSAS cube. This data will be updated in real time when you use it to create a report in Power BI. Every time a user requests data, Power BI communicates with the cube.

Here are some things to consider if you choose to use Connect Live mode:

- Connect Live mode is available for Analysis Services. Analysis services come in two varieties: **multidimensional** and **tabular**.
- An OLAP cube can be accessed immediately by using Connect Live mode. An OLAP Cube is a multifaceted database designed for online and data warehouse application.

APPLICATIONS OF ANALYTICAL PROCESSING [OLAP])

When Power BI is connected to the SSAS cube using Connect Live, it essentially serves as the cube's front-end visual component. To put it another way, Power BI uses the data in the cube to create the report. A direct connection to the enterprise model database is made possible via Connect Live. Multiple people can access the data, and you are not required to replicate or duplicate it. No data model is generated since Connect Live mode doesn't truly import data into Power BI; hence, there isn't a way to modify the model definition.

- The Query Editor is not supported by Connect Live.

HOW TO USE IMPORT MODE TO IMPORT DATA

Use import mode to import data from an SSAS cube into Power BI by doing the following:

- In Power BI Desktop, select the Home tab.
- Select "Get Data."
- Select SQL Server Analysis Service after choosing a database.
- Press the Connect button. The window for the SQL Server Analysis Services Database appears.
- In the Server name box, enter the name of the SSAS server that you wish to import data from.
- In the Database name box, type the name of the database you wish to import data from. The previous step is not required. You will import all of the server's databases if you leave this box empty.
- Click the button for the Import option.
- Press OK.
- Select Windows as the login method when requested.

- Click Connect after selecting the Use My Current Credentials checkbox and entering your Windows login credentials. The Navigator window opens. A list of every table, cube, measure, and dimension in the SSAS database may be found in the pane on the left.
- To view a preview of any of these in the window on the right, click on it.
- Select the measurements and dimensions you wish to include in your report by opening the cube containing them (in this case, Sales Targets), then click the Load button.

CUBE, MEASUREMENT, DIMENSIONS

All of the tables, cubes, measurements, and dimensions in the chosen database are listed in the Navigator window (left), which also displays a preview (right).

The chosen metrics and dimensions are loaded into a data model using Power BI. Keep in mind that the Edit Queries button is active, meaning that the Query Editor is accessible when you receive data using import mode. You can also see the Data and Relationships tabs.

The Data and Relationships tabs and Editing Queries are available in Import mode.

HOW TO USE CONNECT LIVE MODE TO CONNECT TO THE DATA

Here's how to use Connect Live mode to connect to data in an SSAS cube from Power BI:

- Go over steps 1-6 from the last part again.
- Click OK after selecting the Connect Live option button.
- Select Windows as the authentication method when requested.
- Click Connect after selecting the Use My Current Credentials checkbox and entering your Windows login credentials.
- The Navigator window opens. A list of every cube in the SSAS database may be found in the pane on the left. To get a preview of its contents in the window on the right, click on any of these.
- Click the OK button after selecting the cube containing the measurements and dimensions you wish to include in your report.

In contrast to import mode, Power BI Desktop does not connect to the cube. The reason for this is because Power BI Desktop has a direct connection to the data source.

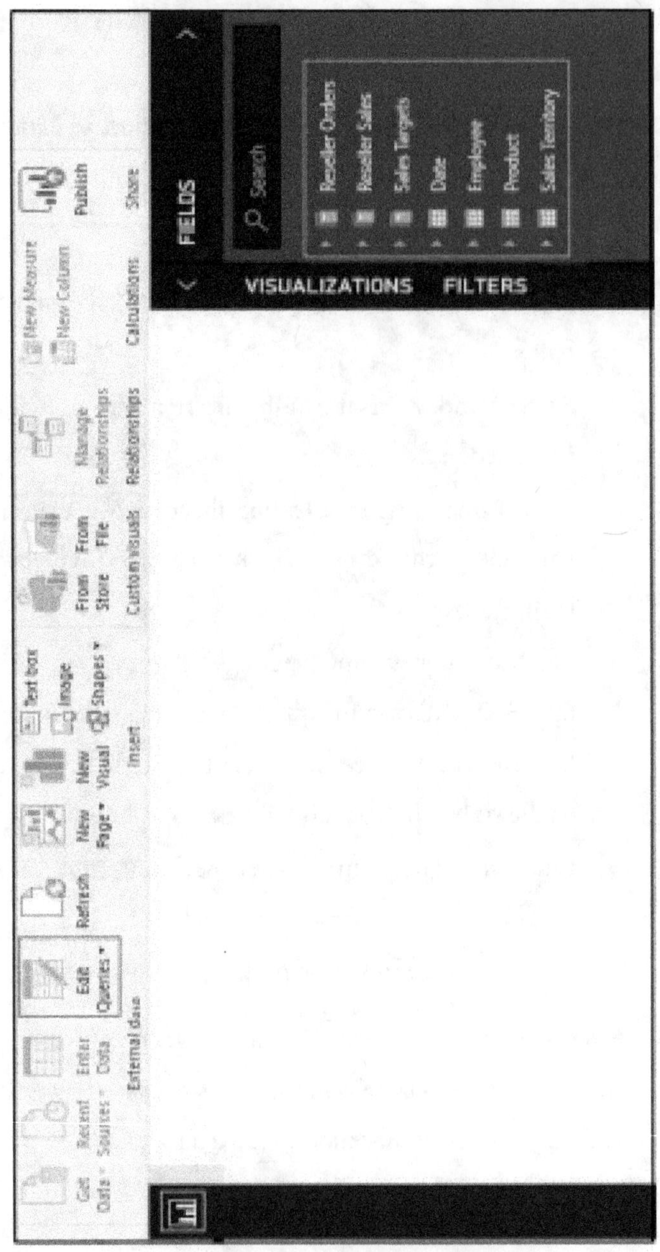
Get Data
Recent Sources
Enter Data
Edit Queries
Refresh
External data
New Page
New Visual
Text box
Image
Shapes
Insert
From Store
From File
Custom visuals
Manage Relationships
Relationships
New Measure
New Column
Calculations
Publish
Share
FIELDS
Search
Reseller Orders
Reseller Sales
Sales Targets
Date
Employee
Product
Sales Territory
VISUALIZATIONS
FILTERS

Additionally, take note that the Data and Relationships tabs are no longer visible and that the Edit Queries option is not accessible.

The following cube, measurements, and dimensions will be included in the report:

- The cube of sales targets
- Dimensions of the product and sales territory
- Measure of Reseller Sales Amount
- Measure of Reseller Order Count

Let's begin with the images. Your report should include the following items:

- **Slicer**: Data will be filtered by category using a slicer.
- **Stacked bar chart**: Reseller sales figures by sales category will be displayed in a stacked bar chart.
- **Map**: Reseller sales figures by region and sales territory will be displayed on a map.
- **A multi-row card**: To display data about associated sales amounts and reseller order counts, you will utilize a multi-row card.
- **Treemap**: The reseller order counts by product category will be displayed as a treemap.

- **A line chart**: To display reseller sales figures and reseller order counts by nation, you will utilize a line chart.

Once the images have been added, you can organize them however you like. The report can also be set up to be viewed on a mobile device, as you saw in earlier chapters. A dashboard produced with visuals from multiple reports is displayed.

HOW TO INSTALL AND SET UP A DATA GATEWAY

As in earlier, you link the SSAS cube and Power BI securely using a data gateway. Power BI reports created from the SSAS cube stay current thanks to this safe connection. The gateway essentially serves as a link between Power BI and the SSAS cube (as well as other Microsoft products like Microsoft Flow, PowerApps, and Logic Apps). Power BI uses this bridge to update reports using information from the SSAS cube.

The system requirements for a data gateway were described above, along with the shared and personal data gateway types that are available. Additionally, it guided you through the process of configuring a shared data gateway. The process of creating a personal gateway was also described above.

You need to configure your gateway to use the Power BI service after it has been set up. Take these actions:

- Sign in to the Power BI platform.
- Hover your mouse pointer over the report you made with information from the SSAS cube under Datasets. Then, click the ellipsis that shows up and select Schedule Refresh.
- The report's Settings box opens. Click the Manage Gateways link after expanding the Gateway Connection section. The window for Gateway Cluster Settings opens.
- Select "Add Data Sources to Use the Gateway" from the menu.
- The page for Manage Gateway Settings appears. After selecting Gateway Name, select Add Data Source.
- Select Live Data Connection under Gateway Clusters. The window for Data Source Settings opens.

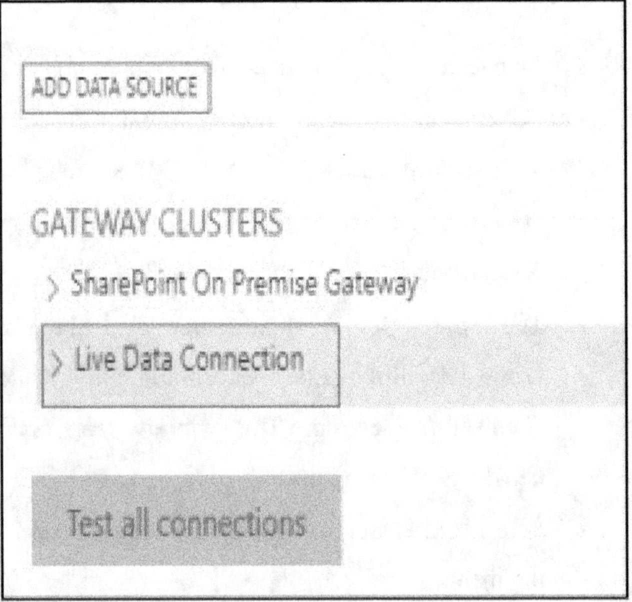

- In the Data Source Name box, enter the name of the data source.
- Select Analysis Services from the Data Source Type drop-down menu.
- In the Server box, enter the name of the SSAS server you wish to connect to.

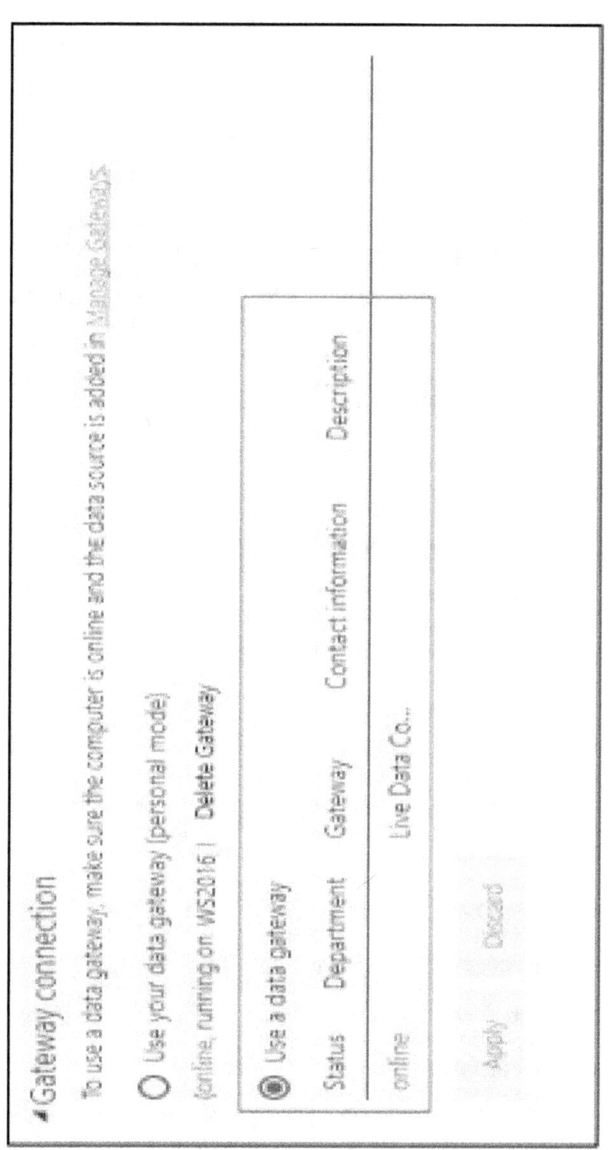

- In the Database box, enter the name of the SSAS database you wish to connect to.

- In the Username box, enter the username for your SSAS server.
- In the Password box, enter your password.
- Select "Add."
- The successful connection to the data gateway should be shown in the Data Source Settings pane.
- Click Apply after choosing the Use a Data Gateway option button in the Gateway Connection section of the report's Settings box. To view the connection's status, expand the Data Source Credentials section of the same pane. Next, configure the data gateway to automatically refresh the report.
- Toggle the Keep Your Data Up to Date option to On in the Scheduled Refresh section of the same window.
- Select the desired frequency of refreshes from the drop-down list.
- Refresh the information.
- Select your time zone by opening the Time Zone drop-down list.
- Select "Apply."

CHAPTER NINE
HOW TO CREATE REPORTS WITH POWER BI USING AZURE SQL

The creation of a Power BI report that uses information from an Azure SQL database as its source will be covered in this chapter. Additionally, you will discover how to configure data refresh functionality for real-time data connectivity.

This chapter includes an overview of the Azure SQL portal and instructions for importing data into Power BI from an Azure SQL database. Establish a live data connection and data refresh functionality. Create a Power BI report.

AN OVERVIEW OF THE AZURE SQL PORTAL

An introduction to the Azure SQL portal is given in this part, along with instructions on how to access an Azure SQL database through the site. Please deploy this Azure SQL database if you haven't already. This database can be found at https://docs(dot)microsoft(dot))com/en-us/azure/sql-database/sql-database-get-started-portal_.

Take these actions to explore the portal:

- In the address bar of your browser, type https://portal(dot)azure(dot)com, then input your login information.

- Following your login, a Dashboard screen containing

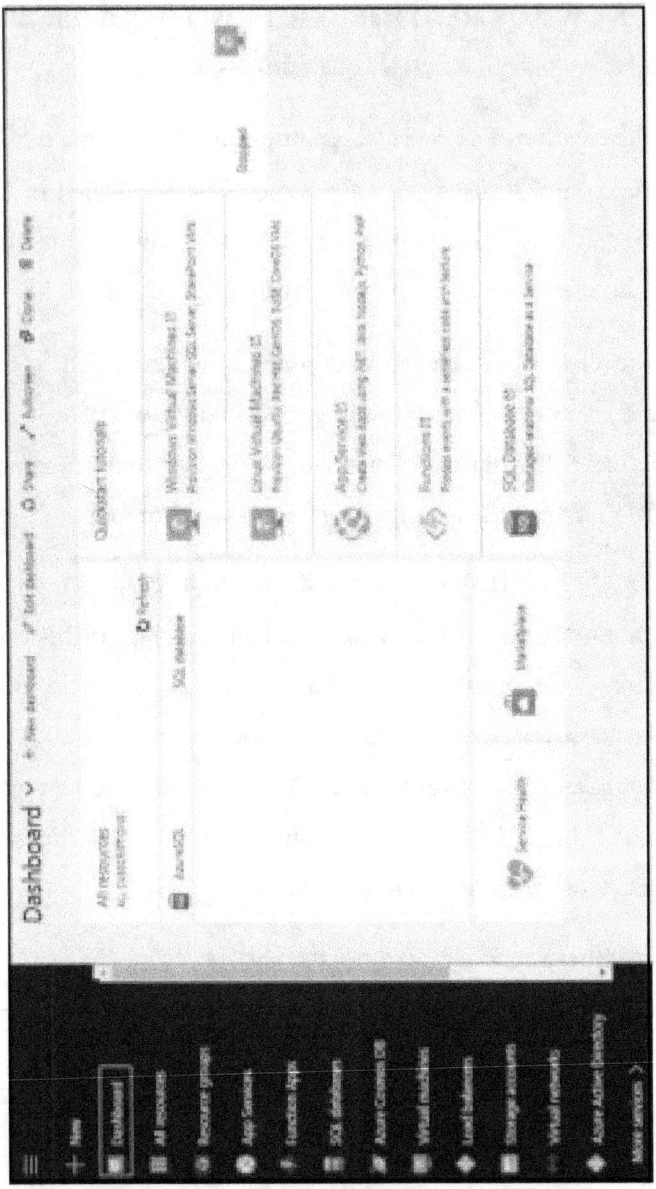

information about your Azure membership and other options will appear.

- Select the SQL Databases option from the pane on the left. All of the SQL databases that are available will be listed in the pane on the right.
- Select a database (in this case, AzureSQL) from the pane on the right. Details about the chosen database are displayed. In the middle pane, you can see that Overview is selected. Consequently, the server name and other general database details are displayed in the right pane.
- Copy the server name as it appears in link form under the Server Name heading since you will need it later when you are preparing the report. Next, click the link. Details about the server, including the server administrator, are displayed.
- When preparing the report, you will need to know the server administrator, therefore make a copy of their name.

HOW TO USE POWER BI TO IMPORT DATA FROM AN AZURE SQL DATABASE

There are two methods for importing data from an Azure SQL database into Power BI, same like when importing data from a SQL server:

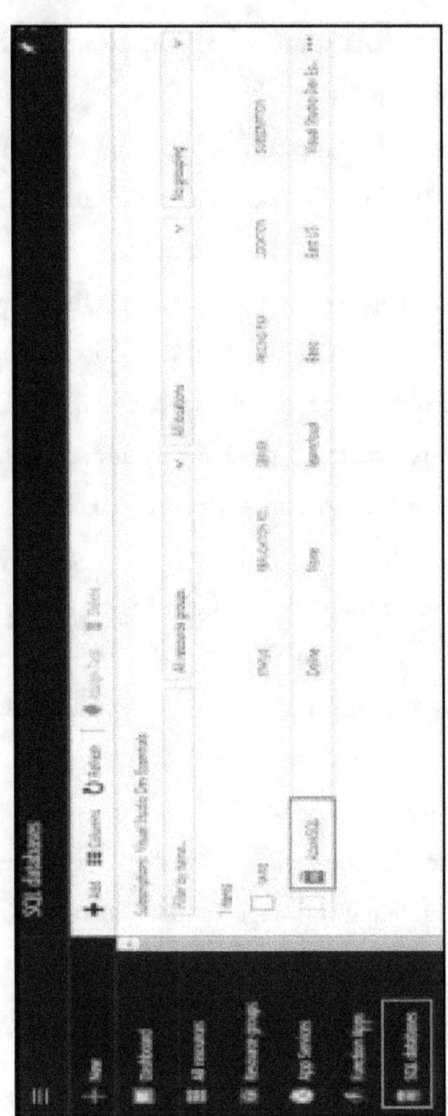

- **Import mode**: Data is cached from the database into Power BI when you import it using import mode. You must regularly refresh the data to make sure you are working with the most recent version.
- **DirectQuery mode:** Data is not directly imported into Power BI by DirectQuery. Instead, it keeps the connection open between the Azure SQL database and Power BI. This data will update in real time when you use it to create a report in Power BI. In this part, you will go over how to import data using both approaches.

HOW TO USE IMPORT MODE TO IMPORT DATA

Use import mode to import data into Power BI from an Azure SQL database by doing the following:

- In Power BI Desktop, select the Home tab.
- Select "Get Data."
- Select Azure SQL Database after choosing Azure.
- Press the Connect button. The window for the SQL Server Database opens.
- In the Server name box, type the name of the Azure SQL Server that you wish to import data from.

- In the Database name box, type the name of the Azure SQL database (in this case, AzureSQL) from which you wish to import data.
- Click the Import button under Data Connectivity Mode.
- Press OK.
- Select Database when asked to specify the authentication method.
- Enter the Azure SQL database's username in the User Name field.
- Enter the relevant password in the Password box.
- Choose from the options in the Select Which Level to Apply These Settings To drop-down box.
- Select Connect. A preview of the chosen table will appear on the right, while a list of every table that is available in the Azure SQL database will appear on the left.
- Click Load after selecting the tables you wish to import. The tables are imported into Power BI Desktop, which uses them to create a data model.

HOW TO USE DIRECTQUERY MODE IN POWER BI

To connect to data in an azure SQL database:

- Repeat the previous section's steps 1 through 6.

- Click OK after choosing the DirectQuery option button under Data Connectivity Mode.
- Select Database when asked to choose the authentication mechanism.
- Enter the Azure SQL database's username in the User Name field.
- Enter the relevant password in the Password box.
- Press the Connect button.
- A list of every table in the Azure SQL database will be displayed to you, along with a preview of the table you have chosen.
- Click Load after selecting the tables you wish to connect to.

In contrast to import mode, Power BI Desktop does not create a data model from the tables it connects to. The reason for this is because Power BI Desktop has a direct connection to the data source.

HOW TO UTILIZE AN INLINE QUERY TO IMPORT DATA

Additionally, you may use an inline SQL query to import data into Power BI from an Azure SQL database. Both import mode and DirectQuery mode imports can be performed using inline SQL queries. You can do an import mode action using an inline query by following these steps:

- Repeat steps 1 through 7 from the "Import data using Import mode" section.
- In the SQL Server Database window, expand the Advanced Options area and enter the following inline query:

```
SELECT Pr.[productid],Pr.[name],
          Pr.[productnumber],
          Pr.[color],
          Pr.[standardcost],
          Pr.[listprice],
          Pr.[size],
          Pr.[weight],
          Pr.[productcategoryid],
             PC.[name] AS ProductName,
          Pr.[productmodelid],
             PM.[name] AS ModelName,
          Pr.[sellstartdate],
          Pr.[sellenddate],
          Pr.[discontinueddate]
          FROM       [SalesLT].[product] AS Pr
          INNER JOIN [SalesLT].[productcategory]
AS PC
```

```
ON Pr.productcategoryid =
PC.productcategoryid
INNER JOIN [SalesLT].[productmodel] AS PM
ON PM.productmodelid = Pr.productmodelid
```

- You can choose to enable SQL Server Failover Support, Navigate Using Full Hierarchy, and Include Relationship Columns.
- Press OK.
- Select Database when asked to choose the authentication mechanism.
- Enter the Azure SQL database's username in the User Name field.
- Enter the relevant password in the Password box.
- Select Connect.
- Click Load after previewing the data columns you specified for import.

HOW TO MAKE A REPORT USING POWER BI

The details of making reports, including adding and organizing visuals, preparing a report for mobile view, publishing and viewing the report, and constructing a dashboard from the report, have been covered in previous chapters. Therefore, I won't repeat that material here. Rather, I'll only tell you which images to include and present the outcomes in dashboard, mobile, and report format. Let's begin with the images. Your report should include the following items:

- **Slicer**: Data will be filtered by product using a slicer.
- **A chart with lines and clustered columns**: Order amounts by product will be displayed as a line and clustered column chart.
- **Pie chart:** The number of customers by nation will be displayed in a pie chart.
- **A donut chart:** A donut chart will be used to display the number of customers by salesperson.
- **Gauge chart**: You'll use a gauge chart to display data about total cities, total items, and total customers.
- **The area chart**: The number of customers by city will be displayed in an area chart.
- **A bar chart that is stacked**: The order quantity count by salesperson and product color will be displayed in a stacked bar chart.
- Informational details like the product name, list price, color, size, standard cost, and weight will be included in a **table**.

Once the images have been added, you can organize them however you like. The report can also be set up to be viewed on a mobile device.

Last but not least, a dashboard compiled from images from different reports is displayed.

HOW TO ESTABLISH A LIVE DATA CONNECTION AND ENABLE DATA REFRESH

Power BI and the Azure SQL database may establish a live data connection. You may maintain the most recent versions of your Power BI reports with this connection.

Follow these steps to set up a live data connection and schedule the refresh of your Power BI report:

- Sign in to the Power BI platform.
- Hover your mouse pointer over the report you made using data from the Azure SQL database under Datasets. Then, click the ellipsis that shows up and select Schedule Refresh.
- The report's Settings window opens.
- Click Apply after expanding the Gateway Connection section and selecting the Connect Directly option button.

- Click the Edit Credentials link after expanding the Settings window's Data Source Credentials section.

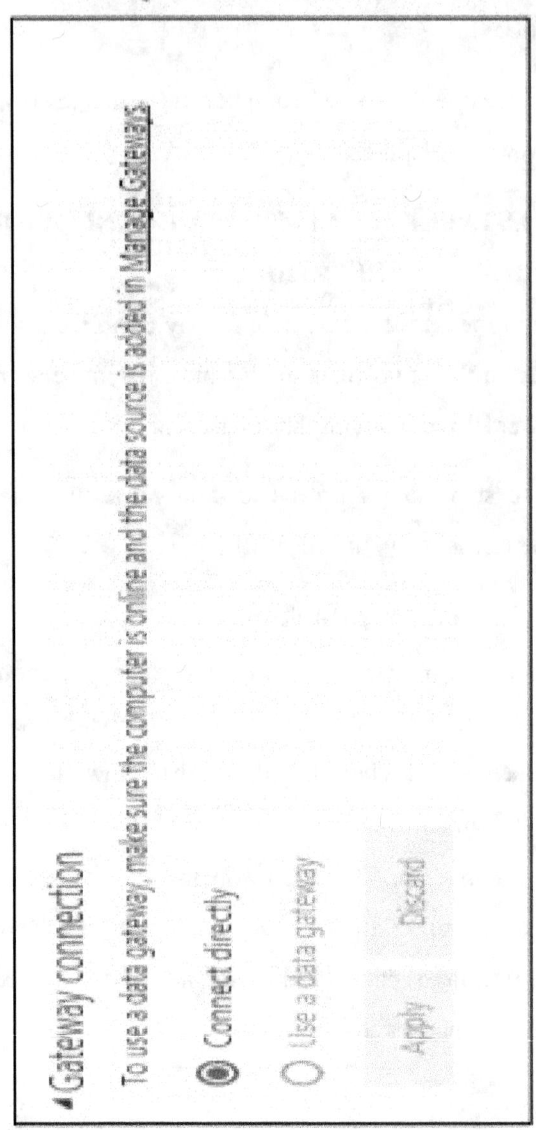

- Enter the name of the Azure SQL Server that houses the database you wish to connect to in the Server box.
- Type the database name—in this example, AzureSQL—into the Database box.
- Select Basic from the Authentication Method drop-down menu.
- In the User Name box, type the username for the Azure SQL database you wish to connect to.
- Fill in the Password box with the appropriate password.
- Check the box to allow end users to access this data source using their own OAuth2 credentials using DirectQuery.
- Press the button to sign in.
- Return to the report's Settings window and broaden the Scheduled Refresh options.
- Select "Keep Your Data Up to Date" from the menu.
- Choose the desired frequency from the Refresh Frequency drop-down list.
- Select your time zone by opening the Time Zone drop-down list.
- If a refresh operation fails, you can choose to get an email by checking the Send Refresh Failure Notification Email to Me checkbox.

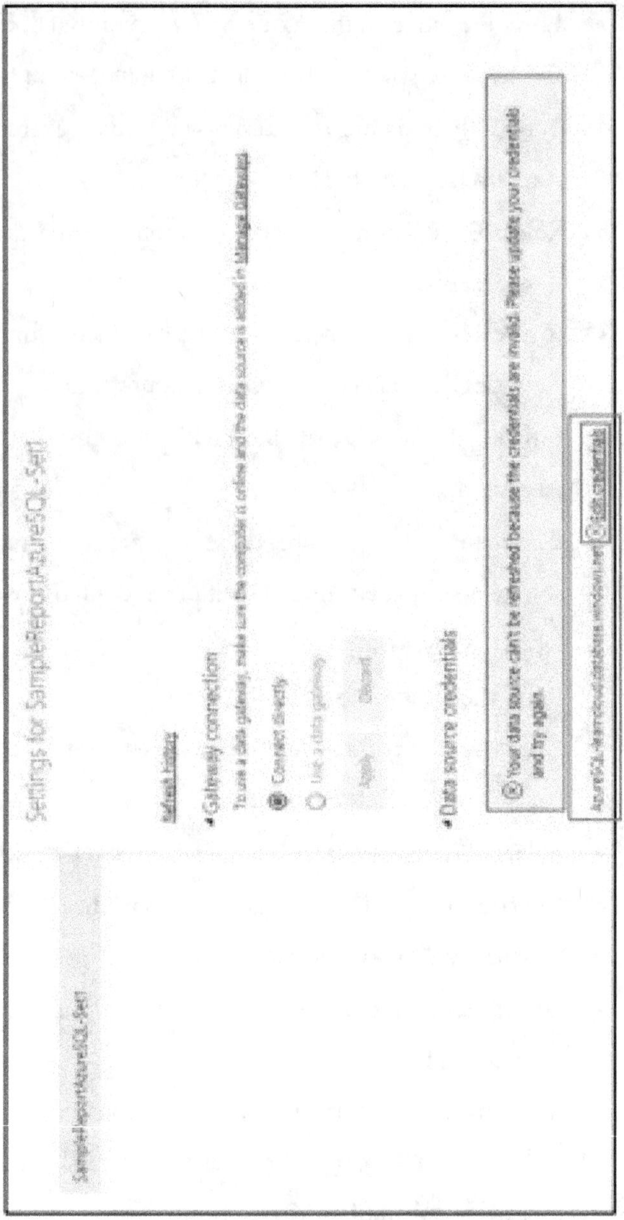
Gateway connection
Connect directly
Data source credentials

- Select "Apply."

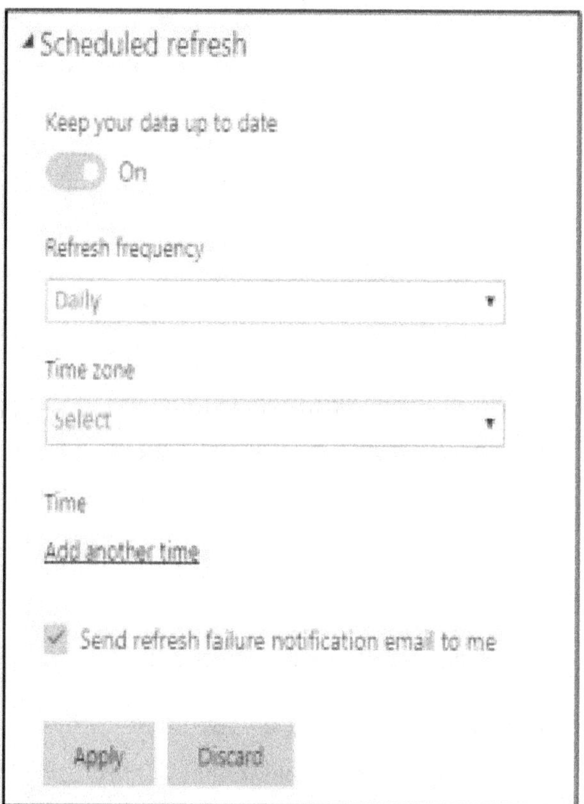

HOW TO CREATE POWER BI REPORTS USING ORACLE

You can import data from an Oracle database using import mode or DirectQuery mode, just like you can with a number of other data sources. In order to interact with the Oracle database, you will also learn how to configure a data gateway. Oracle Data Access Components (ODAC) will be used to configure this data gateway.

Data may be imported into Power BI from an Oracle database in two different ways:

- **Import mode**: Data is cached from the database into Power BI when you import it using import mode. You must regularly refresh the data to make sure you are working with the most recent version.
- **DirectQuery mode**: Data is not directly imported into Power BI by DirectQuery. Instead, it keeps the Oracle database and Power BI connected. This data will be updated in real time when you use it to create a report in Power BI.

HOW TO USE IMPORT MODE TO IMPORT DATA

Use import mode to import data into Power BI from an Oracle database by doing the following:

- In Power BI Desktop, select the Home tab.
- Select "Get Data."
- Click Connect after selecting Oracle Database under Database.

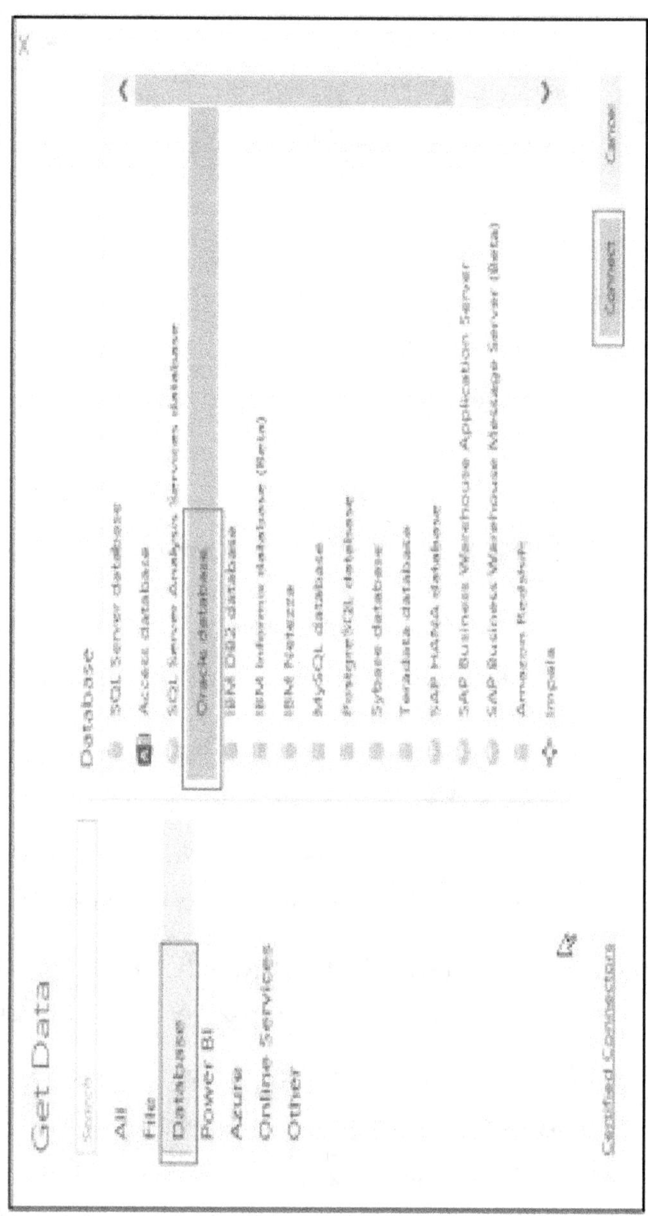
Get Data
All
File
Database
Power BI
Azure
Online Services
Other
Certified Connectors
Database
SQL Server database
Access database
SQL Server Analysis Services database
Oracle database
IBM DB2 database
IBM Informix database (Beta)
IBM Netezza
MySQL database
PostgreSQL database
Sybase database
Teradata database
SAP HANA database
SAP Business Warehouse Application Server
SAP Business Warehouse Message Server (Beta)
Amazon Redshift
Impala
Connect

- Enter the Oracle server name that you wish to import data from in the box for servers.
- Choose Import from the Data Connectivity Mode menu.
- Press OK.
- Select Database when asked to specify the authentication mechanism.
- Enter the Oracle database's username in the User Name field.
- Enter the relevant password in the Password box.
- Press "Connect."

A preview of the chosen table appears on the right, while a list of every table in the Oracle database is displayed on the left.

- Click Load after selecting the tables you wish to import. The tables are imported into Power BI Desktop, which uses them to create a data model.

HOW TO USE POWER BI'S DIRECTQUERY MODE TO CONNECT TO DATA IN AN ORACLE DATABASE

- Steps 1–4 from the previous section should be repeated.
- Click OK after selecting the DirectQuery option button under Data Connectivity Mode.

- Select Database when asked to choose the authentication mechanism.
- Enter the Oracle database's username in the User Name field.
- Enter the relevant password in the Password box.
- Press "Connect." A list of every table in the Oracle database will be displayed to you, along with a preview of the table you have chosen.
- Click Load after selecting the tables you wish to connect to.

In contrast to import mode, Power BI Desktop does not create a data model from the tables it connects to. The reason for this is because Power BI Desktop has a direct connection to the data source.

HOW TO UTILIZE AN INLINE QUERY TO IMPORT DATA

Additionally, you may use an inline query to import data into Power BI from an Oracle database. Both import mode and DirectQuery mode imports can be performed using inline queries. You can do an import mode action using an inline query by following these steps:

- Steps 1 through 5 from the "Import data using import mode" section should be repeated.

- Enter the following inline query after expanding the Oracle Database window's Advanced Options area
- You can also choose to Include Relationship Columns and Use complete hierarchy's checkboxes.
- Press OK.
- Select Database when asked to choose the authentication mechanism.
- Enter the Oracle database's username in the User Name field.
- Enter the relevant password in the Password box.
- Press "Connect."
- Click Load after previewing the data columns you designated for import.

HOW TO MAKE A REPORT USING POWER BI

You will generate a Power BI report in this part using data that has been imported from the Oracle database, which includes HR data, using import mode. I will not reiterate the details of building reports because they have been covered in previous chapters, covering how to add and arrange visuals, prepare the report for mobile reading, publish and see the report, and create a dashboard from the report. Rather, I'll only tell you which images to include and present the outcomes in dashboard, mobile, and report format.

Let's begin with the images. Your report should include the following items:

- **Attribute slicer**: To filter data by department name, utilize an attribute slicer.
- **Slicer**: To filter data by hire date, pay, and job title, you will utilize a slicer.
- **A funnel chart** will display the number of employees by region.
- **Pie chart**: The number of employees by country and region will be displayed in a pie chart.
- To display the number of employees by department and job title, you will utilize a **line and stacked column chart**.
- **Gauge chart**: You will use a gauge chart to display the total number of employees.

Informational data, including the employee's first and last names, phone number, salary, and work title, will be included in a table. Once the images have been added, you can organize them however you like. The report can also be set up to be viewed on a mobile device. Last but not least, a dashboard compiled from images from different reports displayed.

HOW TO INSTALL AND SET UP A DATA GATEWAY

As in earlier chapters, you create a secure connection between Power BI and the Oracle database using a data gateway, which ensures that Power BI reports that are created using data from the Oracle database are always current. Essentially, the gateway serves as a conduit between Power BI and the Oracle database, allowing Power BI to update reports based on information from the Oracle database.

The system requirements for a data gateway were described along with the shared and personal data gateway types that are available.

The installation of a personal gateway was described in prior. If you need assistance installing your gateway, please consult those chapters. (This chapter presupposes that a shared gateway has been set up.)

You need to set up your gateway to use the Power BI service after it has been installed. Take these actions:

- Sign in to the Power BI platform.
- Hover your mouse pointer over the report you made using information from the Oracle database under Datasets. Then, click the ellipsis that shows up and select Schedule Refresh.

- Choose the Datasets tab and enlarge the Gateway Connection area in the resulting Settings window.
- Select the link labeled "Manage Gateways." The window for Gateway Cluster Settings opens.
- In the left pane, select Oracle Data Gateway.
- In the right pane, select the Add Data Sources to Use the Gateway link.
- The window for Data Source Settings opens.
- In the Data Source Name box, enter the name of the data source.
- Select Oracle from the Data Source Type drop-down menu.
- Enter the Oracle server name that you wish to connect to in the box for servers.
- Select Basic from the Authentication Method drop-down menu.
- In the Username box, enter your Oracle username.
- In the Password box, enter your password.
- Press the "Add" icon. The successful connection to the data gateway should be shown in the Data Source Settings pane.
- In the Data Source Settings box, select the Users option to allow other users to utilize the connection.

- In the People Who Can Publish Reports That Use This Data Source box, enter the email address of the person you want to provide access to use the data gateway, then click Add.
- Choose the Use a Data Gateway option button under Gateway Connection in the report's Settings box. Then, choose the gateway (or gateways, if there are multiple), and click
- Install and set up a data gateway.
- A notification stating "Connection Updated" will appear. The last step is to configure the data gateway to automatically refresh the report.
- Open the Settings window and expand the Scheduled Refresh section.
- Turn on the "Keep Your Data Up to Date" feature.
- Choose how frequently you wish to refresh the data by using the Refresh Frequency drop-down box.
- Select your time zone by opening the Time Zone drop-down list.
- Check the box labeled "Send Refresh Failure Notification Email to Me."
- Select "Apply."

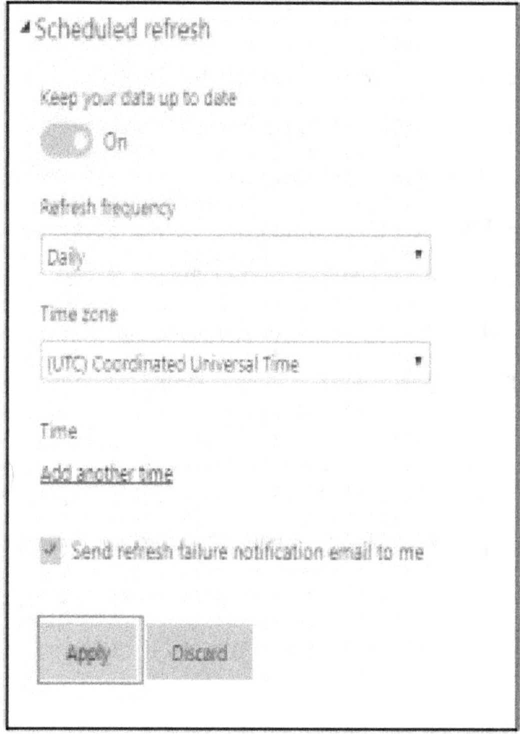
Scheduled refresh
Keep your data up to date
On
Refresh frequency
Daily
Time zone
(UTC) Coordinated Universal Time
Time
Add another time
Send refresh failure notification email to me
Apply
Discard

CHAPTER TEN

Create reports in Power BI using Dynamics 365

This chapter will teach you how to create a Power BI report using Dynamics 365 data as its source. Apart from learning how to integrate Dynamics 365 data into Power BI Desktop, you will also learn how to import it into Power BI service. Additionally, you will learn how to configure data refresh functionality and integrate Power BI reports in a Dynamics 365 dashboard page.

Data importation into Power BI Desktop from Dynamics 365 You need to get an OData endpoint URL from Dynamics 365 in order to connect to it using Power BI Desktop. (A Web API is another name for this.) This URL will be used to access Dynamics 365.

Get the URL for the OData endpoint. Take these actions to get the OData endpoint URL:

- Access your Dynamics 365 environment and log in.
- Select the Settings menu item.
- Select Customizations from the Customization category.
- Select the Developer Resources button. You can see data or download files to create Dynamics 365 apps and extensions using these resources.

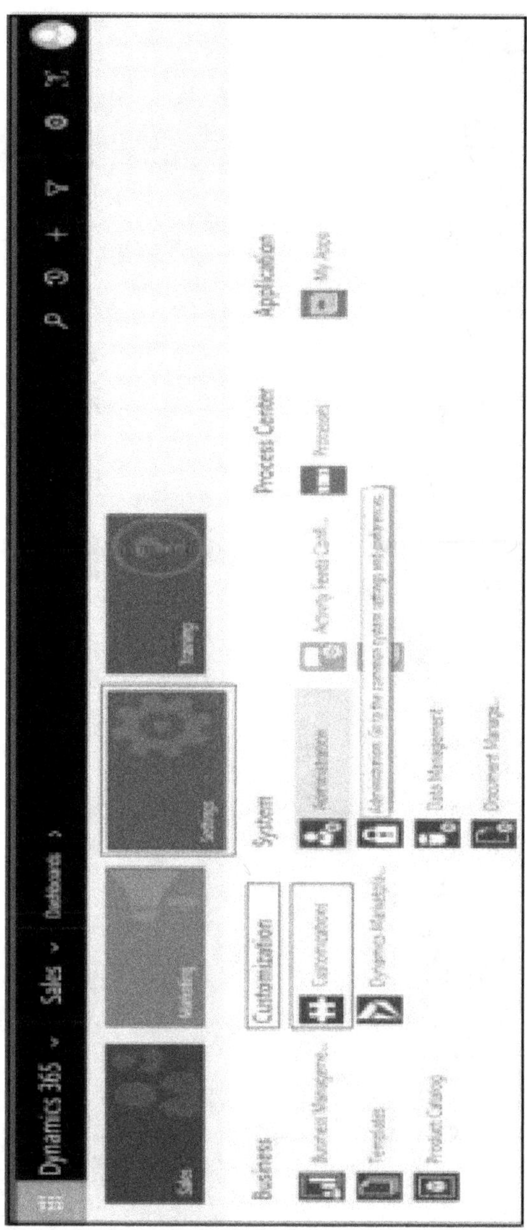
Dynamics 365
Sales
Dashboards
Business
Business Manageme...
Templates
Product Catalog
Customization
Customizations
Dynamics Marketplace
System
Administration
Data Management
Document Manage...
Activity Feeds Conf...
Process Center
Processes
Application
My Apps

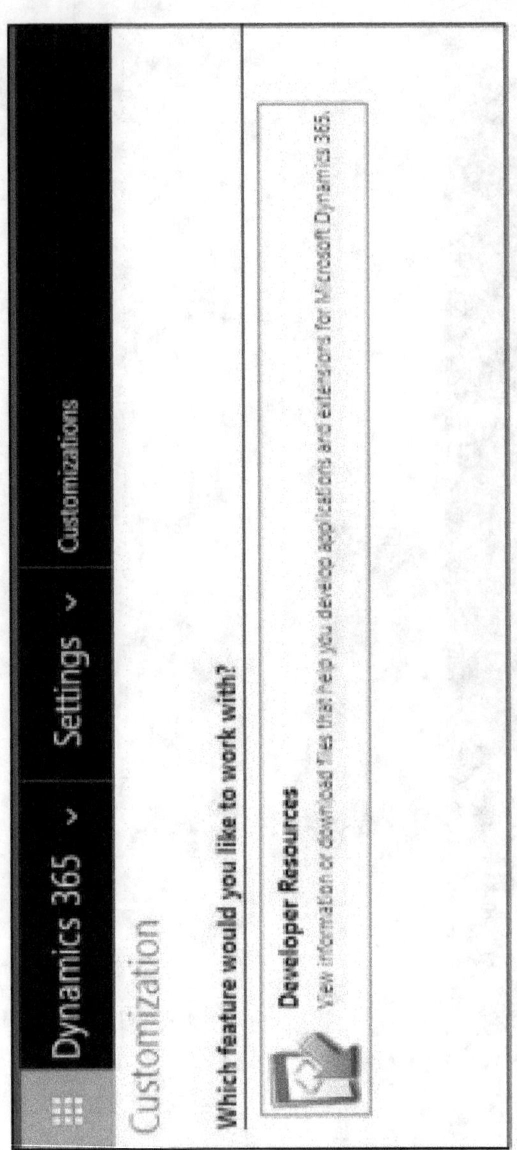

The window for Developer Resources opens.

- Under Connect Your Apps to This Instance of Dynamics 365, in the Instance Web API section, copy the URL into the Service Root URL box.

HOW TO LINK UP WITH DYNAMICS 365

You may now connect to Dynamics 365 to get the data you need for your Power BI report after you have the OData endpoint URL. Take these actions:

- Click the Home tab in Power BI Desktop.

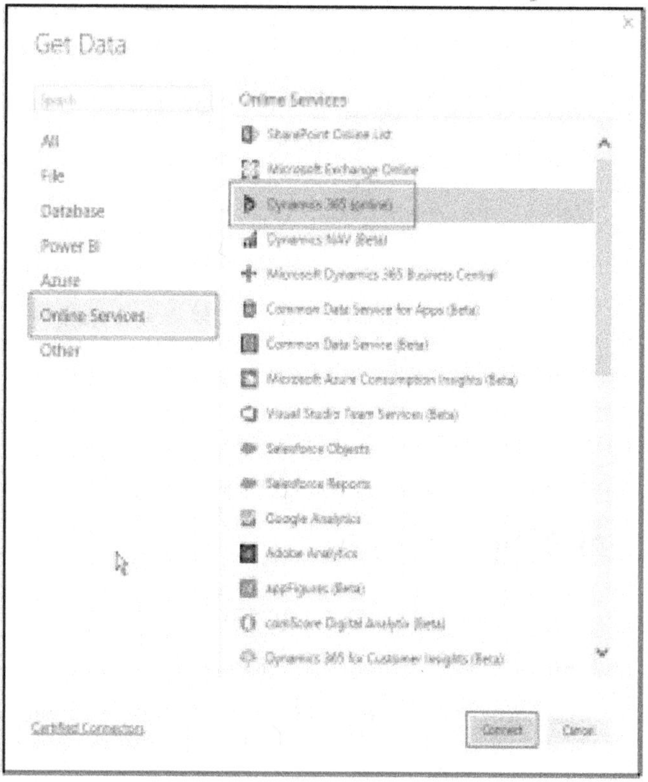

- Select "Get Data."
- Select Dynamics 365 (Online) under Online Services.
- Press the Connect button.
- Click the button for the Basic option.
- Type the URL you acquired in step 5 of the preceding section into the Web API URL box.
- Press OK. This URL will be used by Power BI Desktop to establish a connection to Dynamics 365.
- You are presented with a number of authentication options by Power BI Desktop. Choose Organizational Account in this example.
- In the Username box, type your Dynamics 365 username.
- Enter the relevant password in the Password box.
- Press the Connect button.

Following your connection, a list of every table in Dynamics 365 will appear on the left, followed by a preview of the table you have chosen on the right.

- Click Load after selecting the tables you wish to import. The tables are imported into Power BI Desktop, which uses them to create a data model.

HOW TO MAKE A REPORT USING POWER BI

Using OData endpoints, you will import data from Dynamics 365 to construct a Power BI report in this section. I will not reiterate the details of building reports because they have been covered in previous chapters, covering how to add and arrange visuals, prepare the report for mobile reading, publish and see the report, and create a dashboard from the report. Rather, I'll only tell you which images to include and present the outcomes in dashboard, mobile, and report format.

Let's begin with the images. Your report should include the following items:

- **Slicer**: Data will be filtered by firm name using a slicer.
- **Funnel chart**: The number of employees by job title will be displayed in a funnel chart.
- **Pie chart**: The budget and income by job title will be displayed in pie charts.
- A chart with colored bars, **Clustered bar charts** will be used to display revenue and budget by firm name. Once the images have been added, you can organize them however you like. The report can also be set up to be viewed on a mobile device, as you saw in earlier chapters.

DATA IMPORTATION INTO POWER BI SERVICES FROM DYNAMICS 365

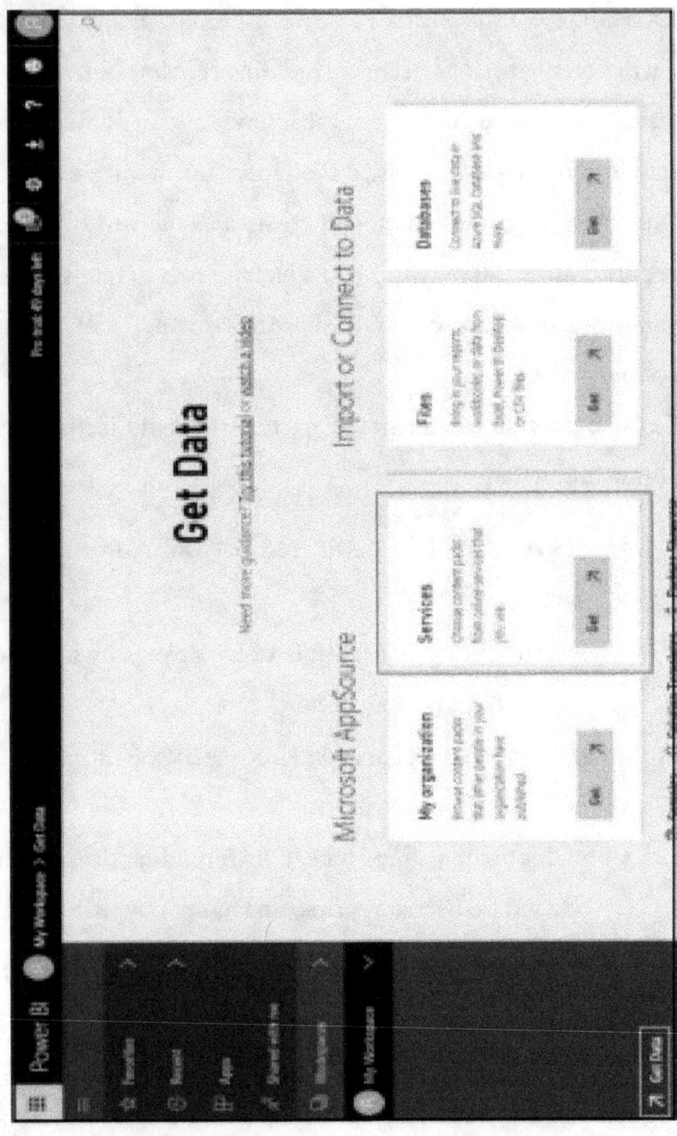

Data from Dynamics 365 may be imported into Power BI service as well as Power BI Desktop. After that, you may use content packs and this data to make unique Power BI dashboards.

Use these procedures to import Dynamics 365 data into Power BI:

- Select the Get Data option from the Power BI service site. Data importation into Power BI services from Dynamics 365.
- Click the Get button in the Services section under Microsoft AppSource. Several content packs are displayed when the Apps for Power BI Apps panel appears.
- To view performance information and historical analytics, select the Sales Analytics for Dynamics 365 content pack. A dialog box titled "Connect to Sales Analytics for Dynamics 365" appears.
- Type the URL for your Dynamics CRM Online Service into the Dynamics CRM Online Service box.
- Type the number that corresponds to the final month of your fiscal year in the Fiscal Year End Month Number field (in this case, I typed 8, for August).
- Select Next.

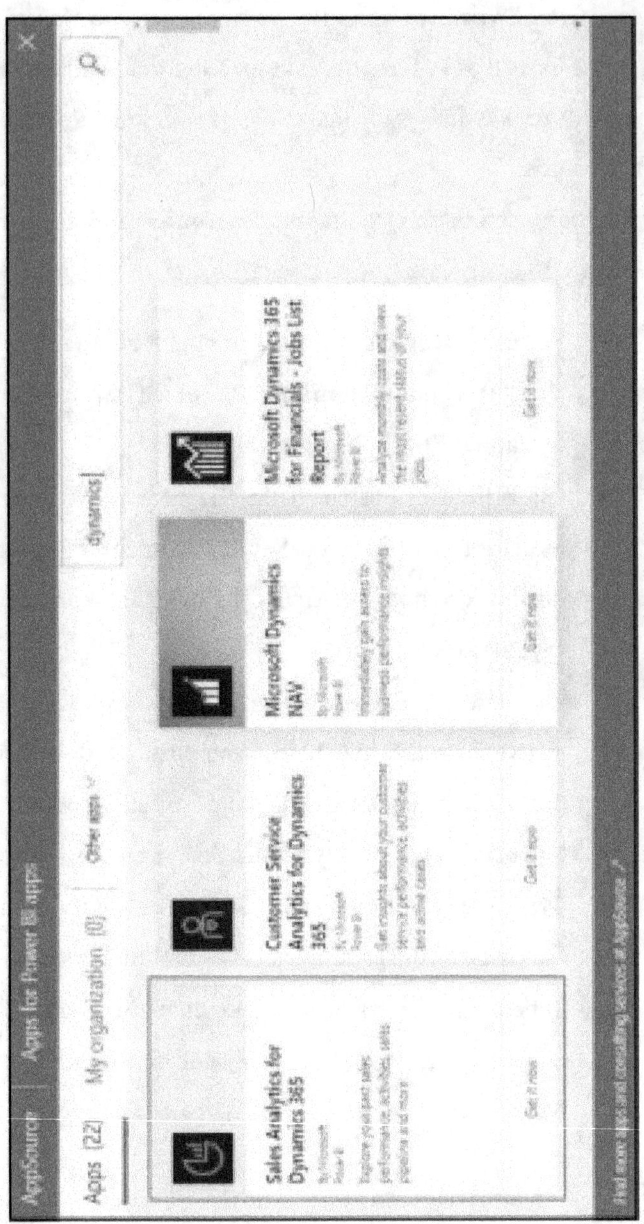
AppSource
Apps for Power BI apps
Apps (22)
My organization (0)
Other apps
dynamics
Sales Analytics for Dynamics 365
Get it now
Customer Service Analytics for Dynamics 365
Get it now
Microsoft Dynamics NAV
Get it now
Microsoft Dynamics 365 for Financials - Jobs List Report
Get it now

Fill in the relevant areas with your username and password when prompted. The specified data appears in a Power BI dashboard.

HOW TO INTEGRATE A DYNAMICS 365 DASHBOARD WITH A POWER BI DASHBOARD.

You can integrate a Power BI dashboard into a Dynamics 365 dashboard, as well as create Power BI dashboards using Dynamics 365 content packs. In this manner, you can get the data straight from Dynamics 365.

HOW TO TURN ON THE EMBED FUNCTION

You must first enable the embed functionality in Dynamics 365 before you can integrate a Power BI dashboard. Take these actions:

- Access your Dynamics 365 environment and log in.
- Select the Settings menu item.
- Select Administration under the System category. The Administration page loads.
- Select System Preferences. You will be able to configure marketing, tracking, and custom settings as a result.

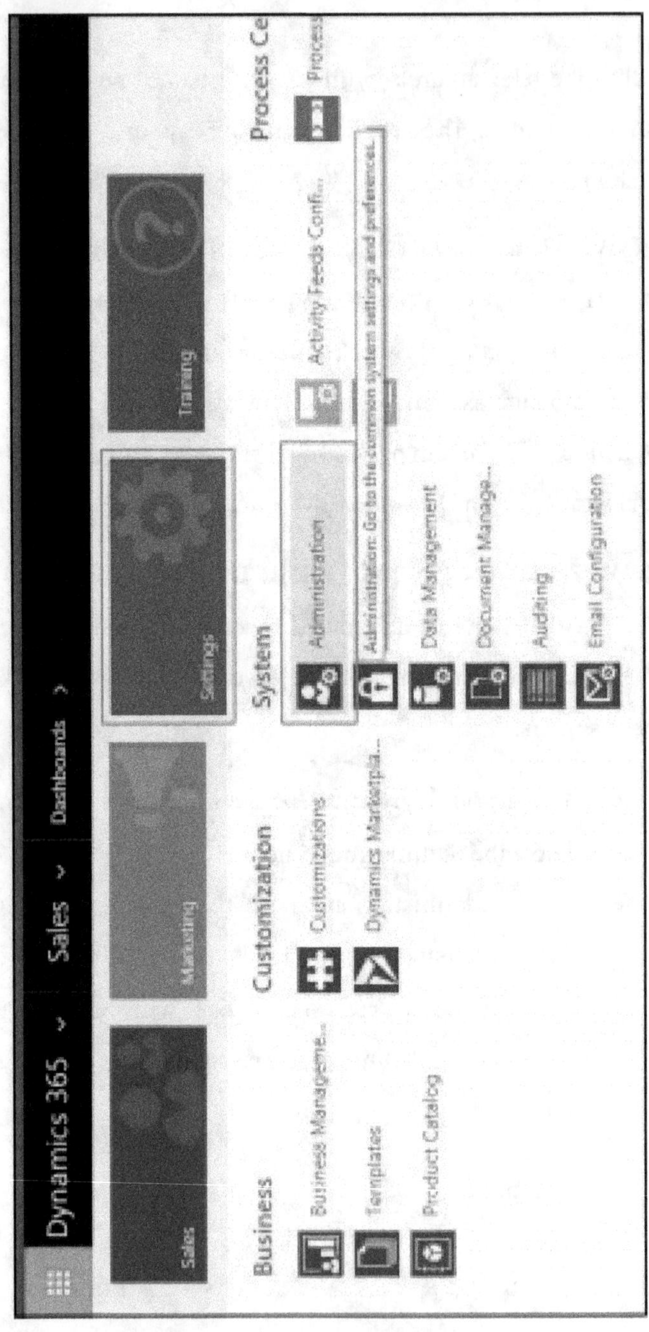
Dynamics 365
Sales
Dashboards
Sales
Marketing
Settings
Training
Business
Business Manageme...
Templates
Product Catalog
Customization
Customizations
Dynamics Marketpla...
System
Administration
Administration: Go to the common system settings and preferences.
Data Management
Document Manage...
Auditing
Email Configuration
Activity Feeds Confi...

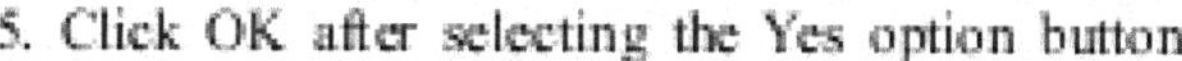

5. Click OK after selecting the Yes option button

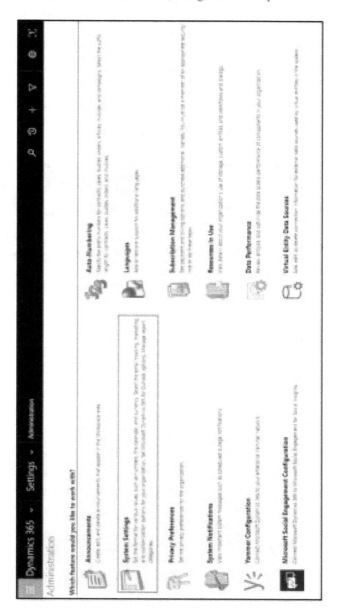

located to the right of Allow Power BI Visualization Embedding. You may now embed a Power BI dashboard into a Dynamics 365 dashboard after turning on the embed option. Take these actions:

- Launch the Sales Dashboard for Dynamics 365.
- Select Power BI Dashboard by clicking New.

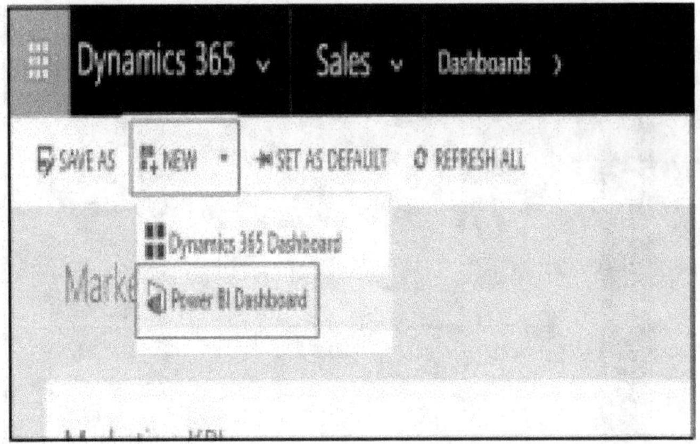

- Select the workspace where your Power BI dashboard is stored by clicking the Workspace drop-down list.
- Select the dashboard you wish to incorporate by opening the Dashboard drop-down list.

- Check the Enable for Mobile checkbox to allow mobile viewing of the integrated dashboard. Click Save after that.

The Dynamics 365 dashboard incorporates the Power BI dashboard.

HOW TO CONFIGURE THE DATA REFRESH FEATURE

It is possible to arrange a refresh between Power BI and Dynamics 365. By doing this, you can maintain the accuracy of your Power BI reports that are based on Dynamics 365 data. Follow these steps to set up a live data connection and schedule the refresh of your Power BI report:

- Sign in to the Power BI platform.
- Hover your mouse pointer over the report you made with Dynamics 365 data under Datasets. Click the ellipsis that shows, then select Schedule Refresh.

The chosen data source's Settings page loads. Expand the Data Source Credentials section after selecting the Datasets tab. Click Edit Credentials after that.

- The chosen data source's Configure dialog box opens.

- Select OAuth2 from the Authentication Method drop-down list.
- Press the icon to sign in.
- Enter your Dynamics 365 login credentials when requested.
- Open the Settings window and expand the Scheduled Refresh option.

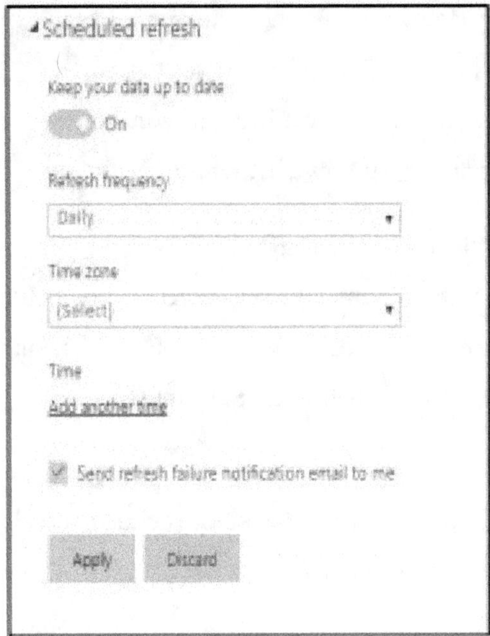

- Select "Keep Your Data Up to Date" from the menu.
- Choose how frequently you wish to refresh the data by using the Refresh Frequency drop-down box.

- Select your time zone by using the Time Zone drop-down menu.
- To get an email in the case that a refresh operation fails, you can choose to tick the Send a Refresh Failure Notification Email to Me box.
- Select "Apply."

CONCLUSION

In this Power BI tutorial book, we have embarked on a comprehensive journey through the essential concepts and functionalities that make Power BI an indispensable tool for data analysis and visualization. From the initial steps of data import and transformation to the advanced techniques in DAX, data modeling, and report sharing, we have covered a wide array of topics aimed at equipping you with the skills necessary to turn raw data into insightful and impactful reports and dashboards.

Throughout the chapters, we've explored the user interface, delved into data connections, and learned how to clean and prepare data for analysis. You have gained insights into the importance of data visualization principles, enabling you to choose the right charts and visuals to convey your message effectively. The hands-on exercises and practical examples provided along the way were designed to reinforce your learning and encourage you to apply these concepts in real-world scenarios.

As you move forward in your Power BI journey, remember that mastery comes with practice and exploration. Don't hesitate to experiment with different datasets and utilize the various features that Power BI offers. Engaging with the

Power BI community, whether through forums, user groups, or social media, can provide additional support and inspiration. Sharing your experiences and learning from others can significantly enhance your skills and broaden your perspective on data analysis.

Furthermore, keep an eye on the ever-evolving landscape of Power BI. Microsoft frequently updates the platform, adding new features and enhancing existing ones. Staying informed about these developments will not only keep your skills relevant but also open up new possibilities for data analysis and visualization.

In addition to technical skills, developing a mindset focused on storytelling through data is crucial. The ability to visualize data effectively will empower you to make informed decisions and drive strategic initiatives within your organization. By presenting insights clearly and compellingly, you can influence stakeholders and foster a data-driven culture.

We hope this book serves as a valuable resource that you can refer back to as you continue to grow in your Power BI journey. Embrace the power of data and let your creativity shine through your visualizations. Remember that every dataset tells a story; it's your job to uncover that story and present it in a way that resonates with your audience.

Thank you for embarking on this learning journey with us. We wish you the best of luck in your future endeavors, and may your analytical skills continue to flourish. Happy analyzing!

NOTE

www.ingramcontent.com/pod-product-compliance
Lightning Source LLC
LaVergne TN
LVHW051437050326
832903LV00030BD/3139

* 9 7 9 8 3 0 7 4 5 5 2 0 3 *